Presenting facts and figures

DAVID KERRIDGE

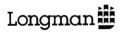

Longman

SERIES EDITOR NINA O'DRISCOLL
WITH MARK ELLIS AND ADRIAN PILBEAM

Longman Group UK Limited,
Longman House, Burnt Mill, Harlow
Essex CM20 2JE, England
and Associated Companies throughout the world

© Mark Ellis, Nina O'Driscoll and Adrian Pilbeam 1988
Published jointly by Studentlitteratur AB, Lund, Sweden
and Longman Group UK Limited, London, England.

First published 1988
New edition first published 1992

ISBN 0 582 09307 4

Set in 9/11pt Helvetica

Printed in Spain by Graficas Estella, S.A., Navarra

Acknowledgements

The graph on page 13 is reproduced by permission of
The Economist and the table on page 35 by permission of
International Management.

Other graphs are based on research carried out by Stuart Wall.

We are grateful to the following for permission to reproduce
photographs; Images Colour Library, pages 5 and 55;
International Stock Exchange Photo Library, page 36; Tony Stone
Worldwide, pages 11 (photo Stephen Johnson), 12 (photo Chuck
Keeler), 18 (photo Tim Brown), 50 (photo Tim Brown) and 52
(photo David Higgs); Telegraph Colour Library, page 27 (photo
Bavaria-Bildagentur); Zefa Picture Library-Stockmarket, page 42
(photo G. Palmer).

Cover photograph by Tony Stone Worldwide

Contents

Introduction   4

1 **Dealing with numbers**   5

2 **Presenting information:
use of signals**   12

3 **Trends**   18

4 **Comparison, contrast and
similarity**   27

5 **Presenting information:
the use of reference words**   36

6 **Forecasting**   42

7 **Cause, effect and purpose**   50

Key   58

INTRODUCTION TO THE LEARNER

Presenting facts and figures is part of the Longman Business English Skills series. It presents and practises the language of facts and figures in a variety of typical business situations.

Objectives The book assumes from the start that you have a basic general knowledge of English and that your aim is to improve in an area of more specialized language. The book has a double function: first, to allow you to familiarize yourself with the language often used when talking about facts and figures, and then to give you the opportunity to practise some of the most useful language.

Contents The book consists of seven units plus a Key. The accompanying cassette contains all the listening material. All material on cassette is marked [🔲] in the book.

Using the book With the exception of Unit 1, all the units are in two parts. Part 1 of a unit introduces the main language point, summarizes it and then gives you the opportunity of listening, speaking and reading practice on the chosen point. Part 2 of a unit shows the new language in the context of a fictional company, Wessex Information, and, again, it gives you the opportunity for further practice. There are also some short writing tasks.

The Key The Key contains the tapescripts of all the material on the cassette and answers to the activities in the units. This makes the book ideal for working with by yourself. Remember that some of the answers are *model versions* and that your answers could be different.

Approach The cassette recorder gives you great flexibility. If you are using this book by yourself, try recording your versions of the spoken practice activities so that you have the opportunity of comparing your version with the model version in the Key.

1

Dealing with numbers

Aims This introductory unit looks at how to talk about numerical data in charts, tables or graphs.

In this unit we will be looking at the following elements:

numbers	15, 50, 15,000
decimals	3.64
percentages	76%
totals	It came to 60,000.
fractions	1/3
mathematical symbols	= +
approximations	just over, nearly
rates and ratios	2:3
currencies	£ FF
abbreviations	kph

Language Summary 1

Listen to the cassette and read the text.

The use of *and* in **numbers** occurs only between hundreds and tens. We say *four hundred **and** thirty* (430) or *one thousand four hundred **and** fifty* (1,450).

Note that American English does not use the *and* between hundreds and tens, for example *three hundred sixty-five* (365).

A number of hundreds or thousands is never spoken in the plural form. We say *four hundred* (400) or *five thousand two hundred and fifty-seven* (5,257).

Listening for information 1

Listen to the cassette and circle the figure you hear.

	A	B
a	17	70
b	230	213
c	343	333
d	50	15
e	280	218
f	19,000	90,000
g	6,000	60,000
h	13,000	30,000
i	13	30
j	6,316	6,360

Check your answers in the key.

PRACTICE 1   How should these population figures be spoken?

1991	
a	Europe	498,414,000
b	Greece	10,041,000
c	France	55,972,000
d	Ireland	3,522,000
e	Italy	57,531,000

Language Summary 2   Listen to the cassette and read the text.

Decimals are indicated by a . *(point)* and not by a , *(comma).*

Numbers after decimals are spoken separately, for example *forty-five point seven three* (45.73).

A zero following a decimal point is spoken as **0** (oh), the same as the letter of the alphabet, for example *three point oh five* (3.05).

Percentages (%) are spoken like this: *sixty-seven percent* (67%), with the stress on the second syllable – *percent*.

Totals: when expressing totals we can say this:
The population of the European Community countries

totalled	
came to	*341.2 million in 1991.*
was	

Listening for information 2   Listen to the cassette and complete the missing information.

Individual country populations as percentages of the total European Community population for 1991.

Belgium	_____
Denmark	1.5%
Germany	_____
France	_____
Ireland	_____
Luxembourg	0.1%
Britain	_____

 **Language Summary 3**

Listen to the cassette and read the text.

Fractions are spoken like this:

1/2	a half	2/3	two thirds
1/3	a third	5/8	five eighths
1/4	a quarter	3/4	three quarters

Mathematical symbols are read like this:

$3 + 8$	*three plus eight*
$17 - 6$	*seventeen minus six*
8×4	*eight times four*
$6 \div 3$	*six divided by three*
$3 + 7 = 10$	*three plus seven equals ten*

$A > B$ *A is* | *more / greater* | *than B.*

$C < B$ *C is* | *less / smaller* | *than B.*

PRACTICE 2 Say (or write out) the following mathematical expressions.

a $95 \div 6$ **b** 17×18 **c** $86 - 17$
d $12 + 346$ **e** $P < Q$ **f** $K > G$

> Check your answers in the key.

 **Listening for information 3**

Listen to the cassette and complete the following extracts.

1 ...turnover went up by nearly _____ _____ to £70,000, and, if we take away the cost...

2 ...nearly _____ _____ of the way home.

3 ... you could divide at least _____ of the work...

4 ...to take two hours. It'll take me _____ _____ _____ by train...

5 ...Nearly _____ _____ of our petty cash goes in photocopying...

> Check your answers in the key.

 **Language Summary 4**

Approximations are particularly useful when describing graphs which are not designed to give exact information but rather to show an overall picture.

Look at the graph of the USA and European unemployment rates and read and listen to the approximations in the comments 1 to 8 which follow.

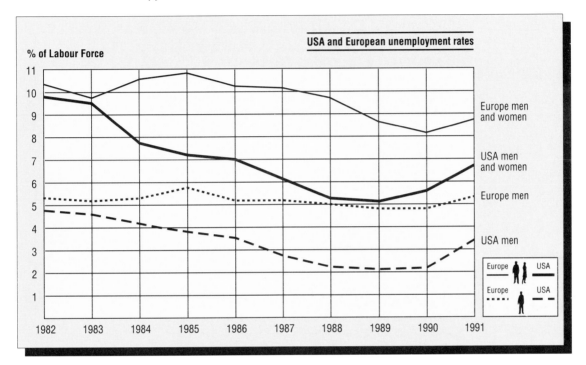

USA and European unemployment rates

1. In 1982 the percentage of the labour force unemployed in the USA was *nearly* ten percent.

2. This figure was *just under* seven percent in 1991.

3. In 1987 it was *approximately* six percent.

4. In 1982 the figure for Europe stood at *just over* ten percent.

5. Three years later in 1985, it was *coming up to* eleven percent.

6. Both figures moved in opposite directions after 1983, USA unemployment falling by *roughly* two percent over the next year.

7. By 1991, the European figure was *more or less* nine percent and the US figure was *getting on for* seven percent.

8. This made the unemployment figures for Europe *well over* those of the USA by 1991.

Focus on Language
Look at the graph again and listen to the commentary on unemployment among men in the USA. Complete the commentary.

The unemployment situation for men in the USA steadily improved between 1982 and 1989.

In 1982 the rate of unemployment stood at _____ _____ percent, but fell to _____ _____ _____ percent in 1984. By 1989 it was _____ _____ for _____ _____ but began to rise around that time. By 1991 the figure stood at _____ _____ _____ _____ _____ percent.

The unemployment rate for USA men was well below that shown for European men during this period. In fact it was _____ _____ _____ _____ in 1991.

> Check your answers in the key.

PRACTICE 3
Look at the graph for European men and prepare a short description of this curve using the following approximations:

just over   approximately   roughly   well over.

> Compare your version with the model in the key.

Listen to the cassette and follow the text.

Language Summary 5
Rates and ratios are usually spoken or written as follows:

*The Netherlands has a population density of 358 inhabitants **per** square kilometre, while that of Spain is only 77 per square kilometre.*

Here is another example.

In 1991 unemployment in Britain stood at almost eight percent; approximately one worker in twelve was unemployed.

This ratio is often *written* as 1:12.

Currencies: spoken currencies come **after** the figure, for example *four pounds fifteen* or *four pounds fifteen pence (£4.15), a dollar twenty-five ($1.25), twenty-two marks (DM22).*

Note the following list of abbreviations of various commonly used rates and ratios.

2:3	= 2 to 3
70 kph	= 70 kilometres per hour
100 mph	= 100 miles per hour
50 kg/sq cm	= 50 kilogrammes per square centimetre
80 rpm	= 80 revs per minute
45 wpm	= 45 words per minute
15% pa	= 15% per annum (per year)
10 kw	= 10 kilowatts

Listening for information 4

Listen to the description of a new electric motor and fill in the details below.

RATE OF MOTOR	
POWER CONSUMPTION	
EFFICIENCY RATE	
PRICE	
ANNUAL DEPRECIATION	
HIRE CHARGE	

Check your answers in the key.

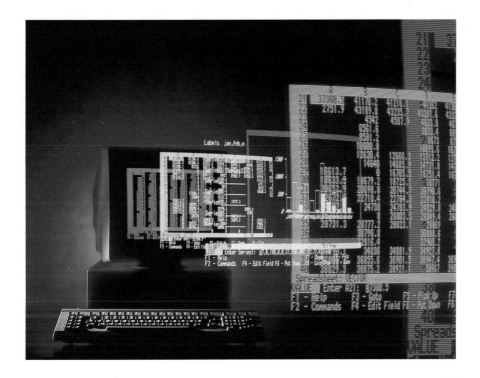

2 Presenting information: use of signals

Aims This unit looks at the 'signals' we use to tell our readers
or listeners what we are going to say or write next.

PART 1

**Language
Summary**

The graph below shows the changes in consumer prices in five major countries between 1988 and 1991. Read the text of a presentation about this graph and notice the use of signals.

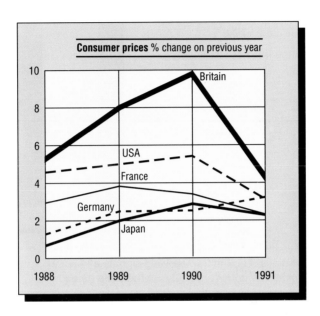

NOTES

*Good morning, ladies and gentlemen. Today, **I'm going to talk about** changes in consumer prices in Britain, the United States, France, Germany and Japan during the period 1988 to 1991.*

Introduces presentation.

***First of all, let's look at** a country whose price inflation was higher than anyone else's during this period.*

Refers to Britain.

***As you can see from the graph,** price inflation in Britain stood at around 5% in 1988, rising to almost 10% in 1990, before falling back to 4% in 1991.*

Refers to visual.

***Now, if we turn to** another large trading country, Japan, we can see that the situation is different. Price inflation in Japan was as low as 1% in 1988, and even though it subsequently rose, it was always well below 4%.*

Changes topic to Japan.

***Finally, let's look** at Germany, the only country experiencing a rise in inflation in 1991. This rise from around 2% in 1990 to over 3% in 1991 was largely due to the extra costs of re-unifying East and West Germany.*

Changes topic to Germany.

***In conclusion,** we can observe that Britain had the highest rate of inflation of the five countries examined throughout this period, although the gap narrowed substantially in 1991.*

Finishes.

Focus on Language 1

Listen to the cassette where you will hear a short presentation about EC, USA, and Japanese steel production. As you listen, write down the signals which are used to:

Check your answers in the key.

1 introduce the presentation;

2 refer to the graph;

3 change the topic to Japan.

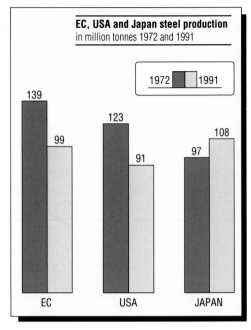

EC, USA and Japan steel production
in million tonnes 1972 and 1991

1972 ■ □ 1991

139

123

99

108

91

97

EC   USA   JAPAN

PRACTICE 1

You have just looked at some signals commonly heard in presentations. Look at the following signals and write them under the correct headings in the table below.

a Finally. . .
b After that. . .
c As you can see from the graph. . .
d Now, turning to. . .
e Now, let's look at. . .
f So, to conclude. . .
g I'm going to talk about. . .

h First. . .
i The aim of this presentation is to. . .
j What I'd like to talk about is. . .
k In conclusion, we can say. . .
l The next. . .
m The graph shows. . .

INTRODUCING A SUBJECT	SEQUENCING	REFERRING TO TEXT/VISUALS	CHANGING A TOPIC	CONCLUDING

Check your answers in the key.

PRACTICE 2

Use the graph on page 13 to give a short presentation on European consumer price changes in the five major countries between 1988 and 1991.

● Give a short introduction.

● Ask people to look at the figures for the United States.

● Change the topic to France.

Compare your version with the model in the key.

PART 2

Background A new market research company has recently started up in Bristol. It is called Wessex Information and its manager, Jimmy Craig, predicts a great future.

Comprehension Check Craig receives a telephone call from someone who is interested in his company's services. Listen to the conversation and then answer the following *true* or *false* questions.

	TRUE	FALSE

1 Coles manufactures guns.

2 Callaghan has read about Wessex Information.

3 Callaghan wants Craig to export anti-personnel devices to Scandinavia.

4 Callaghan needs people to help him sell in other countries.

Check your answers in the key.

5 Callaghan is interested in crime statistics.

Listening for information 1 Later in this conversation Callaghan arranges to meet Craig at Coles' London headquarters.

At the meeting, Craig presents some information on assaults in Nordic countries. Some of it is based on the following table. Listen to the cassette and complete the table.

Sweden		
Year	Number of assaults	Number of assaults per 100,000 inhabitants aged 15 or over
1950	_____	153
1960	8,711	169
1970	_____	332
1972	18,119	328
1974	19,899	360
1976	21,378	386
1978	22,868	411
1980	24,668	440
1981	24,314	432
1988	_____	_____

Check your answers in the key.

Focus on Language 2

Listen to Craig's presentation again and answer the following questions.

1 How does Craig introduce the presentation?

I'm _____ _____ _____

_____ _____ _____ the rates of

assault in the Nordic countries. . .

2 How does he refer to the overhead projector?

_____ _____ _____ _____

_____ transparency on the OHP, we can

see. . .

3 How does he draw our attention to the period 1950–1960?

_____ _____ _____ _____

the period 1950–1960.

> Check your answers in the key.

Listening for information 2

Craig continues his presentation. He now talks about the number of assaults per 100,000 inhabitants in Finland.

While listening, plot the curve on the graph below.

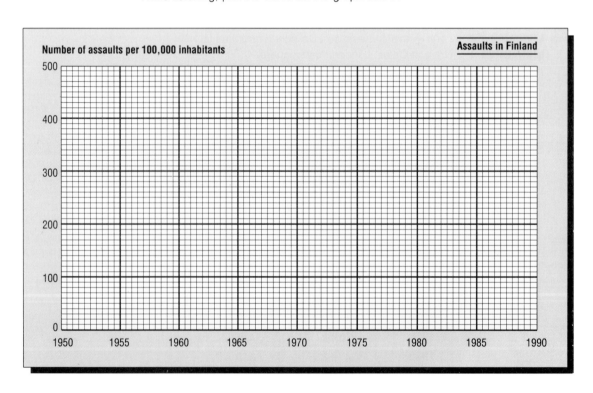

Number of assaults per 100,000 inhabitants — Assaults in Finland

Focus on Language 3

Listen again to Craig talking about Finland and answer the following questions.

1   How does Craig introduce the topic?

_____ _____ _____ _____

Finland _____ _____ _____
assaults per. . .

2   How does he refer to the graph?

_____ _____ _____ _____

_____ your attention to. . .

3   There is another signal which Craig uses to show he wants to go back and talk about something he has mentioned earlier. What is it?

_____ _____ _____ _____

_____ _____ to the Swedish. . .

4   Which of these other phrases could be used appropriately in its place?

   – Now I'm going to talk about. . .
   – The next point is. . .
   – If I can go back to. . .
   – Now I'd like to return to. . .

> Check your answers in the key.

PRACTICE 3

Use the following steps to build up a short presentation of your own. Write out the presentation first. Suggested topic – personal career development/path.

● Introduce the topic.

● Change the topic/direction.

● Return to the topic.

● Refer to visuals.

● Refer back to a point.

● Conclude.

> Compare your version with the model in the key.

3

Trends

Aims   This unit looks at the language we use when talking about trends, upward or downward movements which may be very great or only very slight.

PART 1

Language Summary 1

Some of the most common expressions used to describe trends are set out below.

To indicate upward movement: (↗)

a rise	*to rise*
an increase	*to increase*
	to go up
a climb	*to climb*
a jump	*to jump*

To indicate downward movement: (↘)

a fall	*to fall*
a drop	*to drop*
a decline	*to decline*
a decrease	*to decrease*

To indicate stability and fluctuation:

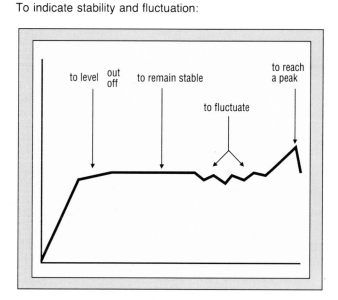

Focus on Language 1

Listen to the cassette and complete the extracts.
Car sales are being compared.

1 . . .the sales of the French motor car companies _____ considerably.

2 . . Renault's market share _____ to about 11% and there was a similar _____ in Citroen's share of the market.

3 . . .did well, with Ford's share _____ to over 12%.

4 Other companies with an _____ in market share included Volvo and some of . . .

> Check your answers in the key.

Language Summary 2

Intensifiers and softeners

The following bar charts show some of the most important intensifiers and softeners which indicate the extent of change.

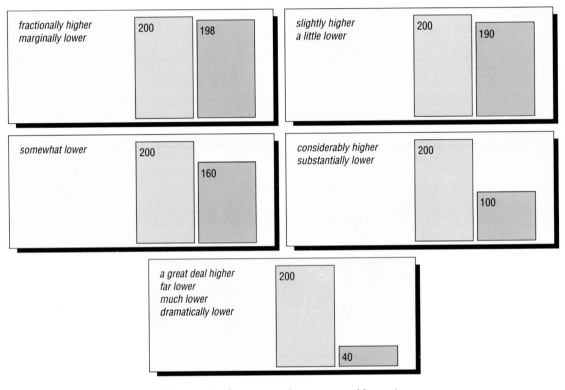

Intensifiers and softeners can be expressed in sentences like this:

Sales were slightly lower
Sales dropped slightly | in the second quarter.
There was a slight drop in sales |

Productivity was dramatically higher |
There was a dramatic increase in | in the Swindon plant
productivity | last month.
Productivity rose dramatically |

Focus on Language 2

Listen to the cassette and complete the sentences. The populations of three towns are being compared.

You probably know that Avonville's population is a
_____ _____ _____ than Bathford's,
but what surprises many people is that Abbotsbury's is only
_____ _____ than Tipworth's population.
Tipworth's population is now _____ _____
than ten years ago.

Check your answers in the key.

Language Summary 3

Rates of change

The following graphs show some of the ways in which the rate of change can be indicated.

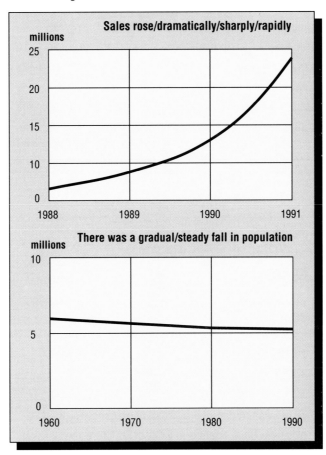

Sales rose/dramatically/sharply/rapidly

millions

There was a gradual/steady fall in population

millions

Focus on Language 3

Listen to the cassette. Two products are being described.

Write down the intensifiers and softeners that you hear in relation to Product A and Product B.

Product A _____

Product B _____

Check your answers in the key.

Language Summary 4

Use of prepositions

Here are some of the most often used prepositions in the context of trends.

*The percentage rose **from 60% to 80%**.*
*The figure fell **from 80 to 60**.*
*The amount stood/stayed **at 234,000**.*
*The figure rose **by** three percent.*
*There was a rise **of** six percent.*

Focus on Language 4

Look at the road accident figures for West Germany (as it then was) and, while listening to the cassette, complete the extracts below.

	1972	'73	'74	'75	'76	'77	'78	'79	'80	'81	'88
Belgium	107	98	90	84	87	88	90	84	85	82	80
Denmark	26	25	19	21	20	20	20	17	16	14	12
West Germany	547	505	462	473	495	523	523	500	514	488	448
Italy	279	276	244	239	227	218	216	230	231	233	215
United Kingdom	360	354	332	333	354	356	358	342	334	333	313
Spain	99	105	99	97	104	107	116	119	112	110	109

Numbers are in thousands

1 . . . the overall trend was _____

2 . . . there was a _____ _____ in the number of accidents.

3 . . . to '77, the number of accidents _____ _____ _____ each year. . .

4 This figure _____ _____ _____ in 1978.

5 . . . accidents _____ _____ _____ 23,000, only to. . .

6 . . . only to _____ again in 1980 to. . .

7 In 1981 the figure _____ _____ to 488,000. . .

8 By 1988, the number of accidents _____ _____ _____ _____ to 448,000.

> Check your answers in the key.

PRACTICE 1

Give a presentation of the accident statistics for the UK.

Look at the table again and write down the trend phrases as well as the numbers and approximations you want to use. Then present your information.

> Compare your version with the model in the key.

PRACTICE 2

Describe the following graph using some of the language introduced in this unit and some of the signals from Unit 2. The graph shows sales of a child's bicycle called the DBM.

> Compare your version with the model in the key.

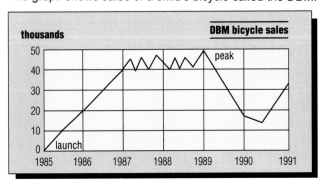

Comprehension   Read the following extract from *Europe in Figures Deadline 1992*[1]. Some of the trend language is in italics.

INDUSTRY AND THE ECONOMY

European industry *remains* a major force in the world economy, and although its share of the European economy as a whole *has dropped*, it still contributes more than a third (37%) of gross value-added: more than in the USA, but less than in Japan. Gross value-added represents the contribution of a given economic sector to the creation of a nation's wealth. Industry's share of gross value-added has *fallen* in all the large industrial countries, and nowadays it is the services sector which has *increased sharply* to provide the largest slice, with agriculture now playing only a very small part. This trend is *most marked* in the USA, but can also be seen clearly in the European Community.

Industrial production in the Community *grew in spectacular fashion* in the 30 years following the end of the Second World War. Since 1974, however, the growth rate has *slowed down* and even registered two slumps in 1975 and 1980–1982, when the knock-on effects of the two oil crises *forced up* the price of oil, industry's basic source of energy. An analysis of the industrial production index shows that the slump in industrial production was *more marked* in 1980–82 in the EC and the USA than in Japan, *where growth continued without any real interruption*. Industry in the EC *picked up* again in 1983, but at a *relatively slow pace*. This recovery was *quicker* in the USA. When industrial production *slows down or falls*, this is generally accompanied by a *drop* in employment, and therefore an *increase* in the unemployment figures. In the EC the lower rate of employment *continued* until 1986–87, while in the USA there has been a *sharp increase* in employment opportunities since 1984. In Japan, employment figures have progressed at an *almost even pace*. In short, industry in the European Community has *lost ground* relatively speaking, to US industry and in particular to Japanese industry.

Now look at the following statements about the passage. Are they *true* or *false*?

1 Industry is increasing its share of the European economy.

2 Agriculture has experienced a decline in its contribution to the European economy.

3 Services have risen rapidly and are now the most important sector of the European economy.

4 The growth of industrial production decelerated after 1974.

5 The growth of industrial production since 1974 has fluctuated less in the EC and the USA than it has in Japan.

6 Japanese industrial production experienced a steady, uninterrupted rate of growth in the early 1980s.

7 If industrial production declines, so too will the level of employment.

8 Employment opportunities have increased more rapidly in the USA than in the EC since 1984.

> Check your answers in the key.

[1]Published jointly by Macmillan Education Ltd, Gill and Macmillan Ltd, Office for Official Publications of the European Communities and HMSO.

PART 2

Background   One morning, Mary Rogers, one of Jim Craig's colleagues
at Wessex Information, receives a telephone call.

Comprehension   Listen to the cassette, in which you will hear the first part
Check   of this conversation. Answer the following *true* or *false*
questions.

1   Vinoitalia is in the drinks business.

2   Tom Johnson is interested in traffic flow.

3   Vinoitalia is based in Italy.

4   Vinoitalia wishes to expand its range in the UK.

> Check your
> answers in the key.

Listening for   A couple of weeks after these telephone conversations,
information   Mary Rogers went to see Tom Johnson at Vinoitalia's office
in London. Johnson had asked her to prepare a preliminary
presentation on the possibility of selling a non-alcoholic
aperitif in Britain to young drivers.

Listen to how Mary Rogers tackles this task and plot the
graph below.

> Compare your
> version with the
> model in the key.

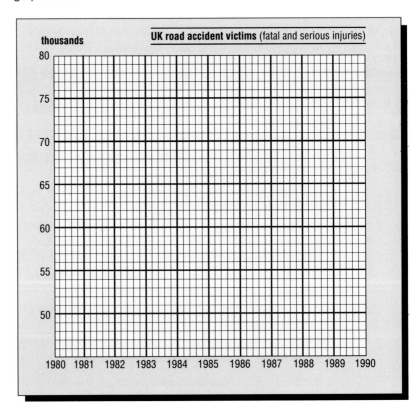

PRACTICE 3 After Mary Roger's presentation Wessex Information got the go-ahead to carry out a market survey on behalf of Vinoitalia. A year later, the product that resulted from that survey – *Cocktail 8* – was on the market.

As you can see from the graph below, sales for the first year did not correspond to the forecast.

Study the graph and then read the interview published in the magazine *Marketing in Wessex* between Mary Rogers and a reporter. Complete the interview.

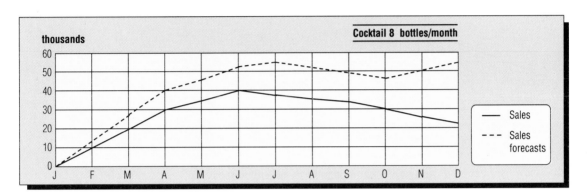

Reporter	*Mrs Rogers, as I understand it, you conducted a market survey. There were no distribution problems, so what went wrong?*
Mary Rogers	*First of all, I wouldn't accept that anything 'went wrong', as you put it. Cocktail 8 was launched in January, and immediately sales 1 _____ quickly, and from April to June this trend 2 _____ .*
Reporter	*Yes, but surely the forecast for April was for higher sales around 3 _____ bottles and isn't it true that actual sales were consistently 4 _____ than forecast?*
Mary Rogers	*Yes, but that's only true for the last month. We'd forecasted a 5 _____ in the summer months because of barbecues, the warm weather. And, in fact, I admit we were overoptimistic, because sales tended to 6 _____ even towards the Christmas holidays.*
Reporter	*So you predicted a 7 _____ of about 8 _____ bottles around July followed by even better sales towards the end of the year?*
Mary Rogers	*Yes.*
Reporter	*So, to return to my first question. What went wrong?*
Mary Rogers	*Frankly, I believe that in the analysis of Cocktail 8 certain factors were not taken into account . .*

Check your answers in the key.

PRACTICE 4 Match the following expressions with the appropriate curve.

a a dramatic rise   **d** steady growth

b a barely noticeable decline **e** a fluctuating performance

c a sudden drop   **f** a stable situation

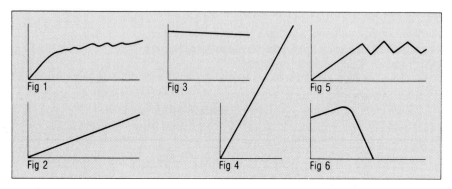

Fig 1   Fig 3   Fig 5   Fig 2   Fig 4   Fig 6

> Check your
> answers in the key.

PRACTICE 5 Rewrite the following extracts from Wessex Information reports, using the form *There is/was*.

1 Production rose by six percent.

2 In Spain consumption is increasing steadily.

3 Sales fell dramatically from 200,000 to 60,000 in one year.

4 It will probably fluctuate considerably this year.

5 1989 saw steady increases in production.

6 The market has been growing substantially over the past two years.

> Check your
> answers in the key.

PRACTICE 6 Describe the following graph using these words: *after that, subsequently, afterwards.*

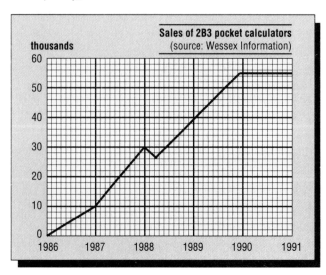

Sales of 2B3 pocket calculators
(source: Wessex Information)
thousands

> Compare your
> version with the
> model in the key.

4

Comparison, contrast and similarity

Aims This unit looks at the language used to show similarity or difference between sets of facts and figures.

PART 1

Language Summary

Comparison

Read these examples of comparison of the population and population density of various countries in 1981 and 1991.

*In 1991 the population density of Belgium was **higher than** in 1981. It went from 323 per square kilometre to 324.*

*Italy's population remained fairly stable during this period at just over 57 million, somewhat **larger than** Britain's.*

*In 1991, the Netherlands had **the highest** population density in Europe – 358 per square kilometre **compared to** only 51 per square kilometre in Ireland, which had **the lowest**.*

Listening for information 1

First look at the chart which shows the number of hospital beds per 100,000 inhabitants in different countries.

Some of the countries have been left out.

Listen to the cassette and fill in the names of the missing countries.

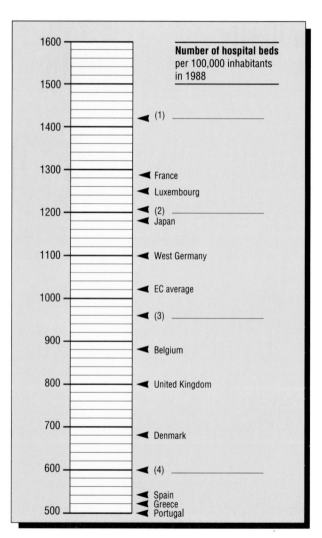

Number of hospital beds per 100,000 inhabitants in 1988

- (1) _____
- France
- Luxembourg
- (2) _____
- Japan
- West Germany
- EC average
- (3) _____
- Belgium
- United Kingdom
- Denmark
- (4) _____
- Spain
- Greece
- Portugal

Check your answers in the key.

Focus on Language 1

Listen to the conversation about hospital beds again and complete the following extracts.

1 The Italian ratio was slightly _____ _____ the Common Market average. . .

2 . . . the Dutch ratio of slightly over 1,200 beds per 100,000 was _____ _____ _____ the average in 1988.

3 . . . in the USA, where the ratio of beds was considerably _____ _____ the Common Market average . . .

Check your answers in the key.

Language Summary 2

Read the following short commentary on the chart which shows the number of hospital beds. Notice the ways in which the comparisons are **intensified** or **softened** by additional words.

*It is surprising that the figure for the United Kingdom is **much** lower that that of Luxembourg, but even more surprising is that the number of beds available in the USA is a **great deal** lower than in either of these two countries. Luxembourg does well. The situation there is **rather** better than in the Netherlands and **considerably** better than in Belgium. Greece does not do so well. It has a **slightly** higher number of beds than Portugal but the figure is **far** lower than the EC average. As for Italy, the number of beds there is also a **little** lower than the average.*

Focus on Language 2

Listen to a continuation of the conversation where the speaker is talking about the situation in the United States and complete the following extracts.

1 . . . in the States is a _____ _____ worse than. . .

2 There's _____ more government control. . .

3 . . . the health service, has a _____ _____ number of beds than a country like Germany.

Check your answers in the key.

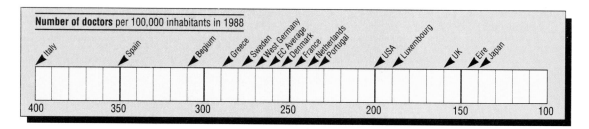

Number of doctors per 100,000 inhabitants in 1988

Italy · Spain · Belgium · Greece · Sweden · West Germany · EC Average · Denmark · France · Netherlands · Portugal · USA · Luxembourg · UK · Eire · Japan

400   350   300   250   200   150   100

PRACTICE 1   Write a short commentary on the chart which gives information about the numbers of doctors per 100,000 inhabitants. Use the model in Language Summary 2 as a guide.

Use these words: *slightly   considerably   a great deal a little.*

> Compare your version with the model in the key.

Language Summary 3

Contrast

When facts or figures are contrasted, the contrast word or phrase underlines the idea of opposition.

Look at these two sentences:
Sales were low last year.
We made a good profit.

The easiest way of expressing this in **one** sentence would be:

*Sales were low last year **but** we made a good profit.*

Now look at these other ways of expressing contrast. They are often used when giving presentations or in written reports.

Although *sales were down by ten percent last year, we made a good profit.*

Despite *there being more jobs on the market, unemployment will rise by two percent next year.*

In spite of the fact *that there are more jobs, unemployment has risen.*

Whereas *inflation went down in Japan in 1990, in all other countries it increased.*

Last year production rose by 11%; ***however***, *this was not reflected in increased sales.*

Last year's trading figures were very satisfactory. ***Nevertheless***, *we mustn't become complacent.*

Other phrases to indicate contrast include:

In contrast (to). . .   *. . . while. . .*
On the other hand. . .   *. . . against. . .*
On the contrary. . .   *. . . compared to. . .*
                                 In comparison (to). . .

🔲 Listening for information 2

First look at the chart which shows the number of televisions per 100 inhabitants in different countries. Some of the countries have been left out.

Listen to the cassette and fill in the names of the missing countries.

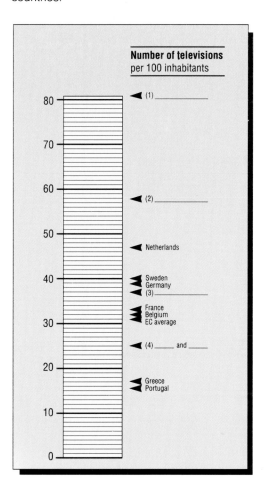

Number of televisions
per 100 inhabitants

- 80 — (1) _____
- 70
- 60 — (2) _____
- 50
- Netherlands
- 40 — Sweden / Germany / (3) _____
- France / Belgium / EC average
- 30
- (4) _____ and _____
- 20
- Greece / Portugal
- 10
- 0

Check your answers in the key.

🔲 Focus on Language 3

Listen to the cassette again and complete the following extracts.

1 For example, _____ Denmark is a relatively small country...

2 And then, _____ its reputation for technology, the ratio for Japan...

3 Italy had many more channels than Ireland; _____, they both had a ratio...

4 ...per hundred, _____, unsurprisingly, the USA was...

Check your answers in the key.

PRACTICE 2 Write a a short paragraph about the numbers of cars per 100 inhabitants in the countries named on the chart.

Use some of the following words: *whereas   compared to while   despite   although.*

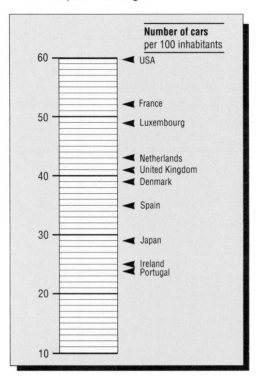

> Compare your version with the model in the key.

Language Summary 4

Similarity

We can express similarity in several ways:

*The steel industries of **both** Britain and France are facing a difficult period.*

***Like** most other European countries, Germany has a well-established social security system.*

*Tourism in Greece has increased dramatically in the last few years. **The same** is true for other Mediterranean countries.*

*The British government's attitude to solving unemployment **is similar to** that of the US government.*

***Neither** the British **nor** the other European Community countries wish to set up high tariff barriers against Far Eastern imports for fear of retaliation.*

*Ireland has a rather low number of cars per 100 inhabitants – the precise figure is 25 cars for every 100 people.
Similarly, Japan with a ratio of 29 cars to every 100 people has a relatively low number of cars on its roads.*

 **Focus on Language 4**

First look at the table which gives information about the numbers of telephones per 100 inhabitants in different countries. Then listen to the cassette and complete the following extracts.

Phones per 100 inhabitants 1988	
Sweden	89
USA	87
Spain	36
Greece	34
Portugal	21
Ireland	23
Japan	56
UK	57
Germany	63
Italy	46
France	53

1 . . . but _____ Sweden and the USA had getting. . .

2 . . . the ratio for Spain was _____ _____ Greece . . .

3 . . . rather _____ Ireland, in fact.

> Check your answers in the key.

PRACTICE 3 Using the same chart about the number of telephones, prepare a short presentation about Germany, the UK, Spain, Ireland and Portugal.

> Compare your version with the model in the key.

PRACTICE 4 Divorce rates per 1,000 marriages

1972	'73	'74	'75	'76	'77	'78	'79	'80	'81	'84	'88
West Germany	87	90	99	107	108	75	32	79	96	110	173	272
Italy	33	18	18	11	12	11	10	11	12	11	31	61
United Kingdom	125	114	121	129	136	138	153	148	160	157	229	338

The following text refers to the table above. Complete it, using the following words: *although   similarly in contrast   however   while.*

If we take the first five years, till 1976 that is, we can see that **1** _____ the divorce rate in Britain and Germany rose, that of Italy fell from 33 to 12 per thousand marriages. **2** _____, the following years, '76 to '78, saw a sharp fall in Germany's divorce rate – from 108 to 32 per thousand. Italy, **3** _____, continued to experience a drop in the divorce rate in the same period, the figure going down by a further two per thousand. **4** _____, divorces in Britain continued to rise, reaching 153 per thousand in 1978. Germany's rate went up from 75 per 1,000 in 1977 to 110 in '81, **5** _____ it did fall in 1978. Since 1981, there has been a rapid and continuous rise in the divorce rate in all three countries.

> Check your answers in the key.

PART 2

Background Voltomatico is the Spanish subsidiary of a US electronics firm and is situated in a rural area. The company has been considering policy changes involving work patterns.

Garcia Llinares, Voltomatico's Personnel Manager, is meeting his US director soon and must present a report of his recommendations for alternative work patterns. However, he lacks adequate background and statistical information.

One morning, he was leafing through a magazine and the following paragraphs in an article caught his eye.

Comprehension Read the extract carefully and say if the statements are *true* or *false*.

Swedish and Dutch firms prove to be the most experimental in trying out most of the alternative work patterns. Companies from both countries, however, show the highest resistance in the survey towards sabbaticals.

Swiss firms, on the other hand, make the most use of sabbaticals and homebased workers. The shorter working week is most widely practised in Belgium, where there is relatively little interest in such things as phased retirement and job sharing.

French and German firms show relatively high usages of flexible working hours but have very little interest in either job sharing or the shorter working week. Early or late retirement schemes are most widely practised in UK firms and least popular in Danish firms. Many of the practices remain virtually untried in Spain and Italy.

However, even Italian and Spanish managers are in accord with their European counterparts on the practical need for corporations to introduce changes in working patterns.

Companies are going to have to adapt their future working patterns to cope "with a shortage of conventional manpower due to an older population and reduced birth rate," observes a Spanish manager. "Workers are looking for more humane and worthwhile jobs", adds an Italian manager.

There is also broad agreement among respondents on the main pressures that will induce changes in future working patterns. Of the total, 58.8% cite rising unemployment as the primary factor; while 57.4% cite worker demands for more leisure and more convenient working hours.

---

1 Although the Swedes and Dutch experiment with some ideas, they reject others.

2 The Swiss are similar to the Swedes and Dutch in their work patterns.

3 The Belgians have a shorter working week and favour early retirement.

4 Early retirement is most common in the UK.

5 Early retirement isn't very common in Denmark.

6 Spanish managers aren't ready to introduce new practices.

7 Rising unemployment isn't the only thing that will help create new work patterns.

Check your answers in the key.

PRACTICE 5 The following day Garcia Llinares telephoned Wessex Information. He was very interested in the idea of flexible working hours. Jim Craig's name had been given to him and Llinares wanted Wessex to get some statistics on flexible working hours.

The following statistics are those Jim Craig located. Study the statistics for France and Spain. Then complete the extract from the report which Llinares wrote for his US director, using the words and phrases given.

	Base	Has not tried and has no plans to try	Has tried	Plans to try within next five years	Plans to enlarge the programme*	Plans to maintain the programme at it's present level*	Dropped the programme or has plans to drop it*
Germany	90	20.0%	67.8%	5.6%	14.8%	83.6%	1.6%
Italy	86	32.6%	50.0%	17.4%	18.6%	76.7%	4.7%
Belgium	107	29.0%	56.1%	14.0%	10.0%	85.0%	3.3%
France	62	17.7%	74.2%	8.1%	39.1%	60.9%	0%
Spain	70	38.6%	48.6%	10.0%	2.9%	88.2%	8.8%
Sweden	95	14.7%	68.3%	13.7%	12.7%	88.7%	0%
Netherlands	86	19.8%	68.6%	11.6%	8.5%	84.7%	3.4%
UK	125	33.6%	45.6%	12.8%	14.0%	71.9%	14.0%
Denmark	83	20.5%	60.2%	15.7%	24.0%	76.0%	0%
Switzerland	92	15.2%	68.5%	10.9%	14.3%	84.1%	1.6%

FLEXIBLE WORKING HOURS

* Calculated as a percentage of those firms that have tried flexible working hours.
Totals add up to less than 100% because those who did not answer have been omitted.

against   compared to   whereas   in contrast to

France and Spain, as you can see, show considerable differences. **1** _____ nearly 75% of French respondents had tried flexitime, this was the case in only about 50% of Spanish respondents. **2** _____ French companies, a very large number of Spanish companies had no intention of trying out the programme. The high percentage of Spanish respondents with no plan to change the level of the programme (88.2%) is **3** _____ the 39% of French companies which plan to enlarge their programme. Perhaps the most significant contrast is between those who have dropped or will drop the programme: 8.8% in Spain **4** _____ 0% in France.

Check your answers in the key.

PRACTICE 6 Now write a report on the UK and Switzerland, using the statistics in the table above.

Compare your version with the model in the key.

5 Presenting information: the use of reference words

Aims   This unit looks at the use of reference words like *this*, *it* and *which*, whose correct use is essential to avoid repetition.

PART 1

**Language
Summary**

Look at the table on population density, then read the text which follows it. Notice what the words in italics refer to.

	POPULATION DENSITY Inhabitants per square kilometre	
	1972	1988
Belgium	318	324
West Germany	248	247
France	95	103
Ireland	43	52
Italy	181	191
Spain	68	77
EC average	159	165
Japan	281	325
The Netherlands	324	358

The first country is Belgium and we can see that *its* population density went from 318 to 324 inhabitants per square kilometre, quite a jump compared to West Germany *whose* population density stayed almost the same. *That* of France rose sharply from 95 to 103 and Ireland's rose similarly. Italy and Spain experienced a higher growth than the EC average *which* was of six inhabitants per square kilometre. *They* had a rise of ten and nine respectively. *This* may well have some effect on future housing policies in these two countries.

The country with the biggest growth in population density is Japan. *It* shot up from 281 to 325 in 1988. However, the Netherlands is not far behind, with a rise of 34 inhabitants per square kilometre in this period.

its refers to Belgium.

whose refers to West Germany.
That refers to France's population density.

which refers to the EC average.
They refers to Italy and Spain.
This refers to Italy and Spain's rise.

It refers to Japan's population density.

Focus on Language 1

Listen to the conversation between Scott, an American, and Werner, his German business acquaintance. Then answer the following questions. Scott speaks first.

What do the words in italics refer to?

1 ... *its* own premises...

2 ... *it* will pay off...

3 ... *they* like?

4 ... *which* you can...

PRACTICE 1

The following bar graph shows imports as a percentage of GDP (Gross Domestic Product) in the countries mentioned in 1981 and 1989. Complete the commentary below it, using reference words.

> Check your answers in the key.

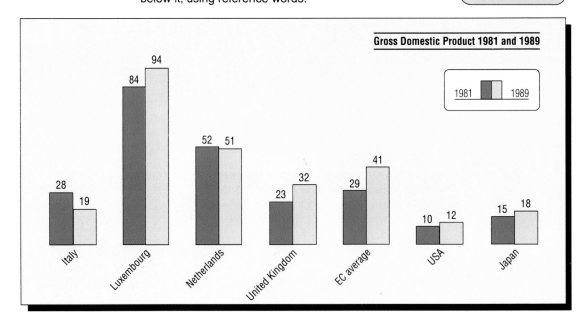

Gross Domestic Product 1981 and 1989

The United Kingdom's level of imports as a percentage of GDP rose to over 30% in 1989, in common with many of **1** _____ European neighbours. However, **2** _____ of Luxembourg outdistanced all **3** _____ competitors with nearly 95% in 1989. The Netherlands, **4** _____ rate was far lower than **5** _____ of Luxembourg, stood at about 51% in 1989. In that year Italy's rate dropped to about 19%, well below **6** _____ 1981 rate. The average EC rate rose by about 12% over the period in question, much higher than for the USA and Japan. But even **7** _____ countries experienced a rise in imports against GDP, the USA by 2% and Japan by 3%.

> Check your answers in the key.

Comprehension 1 Read the extract from a magazine article and answer the questions which follow. (The words in ***bold italics*** relate to question B below.)

An executive life-style, for the spouse at least, is no bed of roses, our 13-country survey reveals

Behind every great man, runs the cliché, is a woman, though in these days of sexual equality perhaps *it* should be behind every person is another person.

There is little doubt that the cliché still holds good for most senior executives. Committed to jobs that demand long hours and frequent absences from home, ***they*** rely heavily on someone, and ***it*** is still overwhelmingly a wife, to maintain their domestic base, run their personal affairs and bring up their children.

A 13-country survey – not of senior executives but of their wives and husbands by *International Management* – shows how far that reliance and dependence on spouses goes. In general, perhaps luckily for business, ***they*** get the support they ask for. But it is not always given willingly. And there are a number of areas of complaint. In one or two cases real loneliness and distress peep through the anonymous statistics.

Randomly selected readers of *International Management* were asked to pass on a confidential questionnaire to their spouses. The answers show some surprising and unexpected discrepancies between the regions of the world surveyed.

For example, in families where only one partner worked, one question asked whether the spouses felt they had sacrificed their career for ***that*** of their partners. Predictably, there was a high feeling of sacrifice in Sweden (33.3%), but the highest figures came from three Asian countries, Hong Kong, Japan and Singapore, where respectively 42.1%, 40.8% and 50% feel ***they*** sacrificed their career compared with a worldwide figure of only 26%.

Intriguingly, though, 77.8% of respondents in Singapore said they had made the sacrifice willingly, compared with a world average of just over 50%. Only in Britain, Hong Kong and Japan were careers given up 'very reluctantly'.

Apart from career, the other sacrifices involved in being married to an executive ***that*** were most mentioned were family roots (22.8%), social life (22.7%), and hobbies and interests (20.2%).

Travel and foreign relocations figure highly as the banes of the executives' spouses' lives.

'Staying at home while he travels' was one sacrifice noted by a US respondent while a German spouse pointed to the problems of adapting to different countries. Not having a permanent home was the sacrifice mentioned by one Japanese respondent.

In general the sacrifices are thought to be worthwhile, 72% of all questioned agreeing with ***this*** (in Hong Kong the figure was 100%) and only 7.7% disagreeing. A hefty 20.3%, however, gave no answer to this question.

A Say whether these sentences are true or false.

1 In general, spouses' help is given willingly.

2 Spouses in Asia feel they have sacrificed their careers more than those in Europe.

3 All respondents in Singapore gave up their careers reluctantly.

4 In Britain, careers are given up more reluctantly than in Singapore.

B Say what the words in ***bold italics*** refer to.

> Check your answers in the key.

PRACTICE 2 Put the following reference words into the sentences below:
which this each both who it.

We looked at three projects, **1** _____ costing more than £2 million.

Italy and France did well. **2** _____ produced more than the previous year.

The result was not just poor. **3** _____ was the worst for years.

The Personnel manger, **4** _____ wrote the report **5** _____ caused the problem, has resigned.

6 _____ was completely unexpected.

Check your answers in the key.

PART 2

Background In this section we again refer to the Spanish company, Voltomatico, introduced in Unit 4.

Comprehension 2 Below is another extract from Linares' report to his US director. Read it and answer the questions which follow. The numbers on the right refer to exercise **B**.

. . . so after a preliminary telephone contact with Craig, we met in London to discuss the question of flexitime for Volomatico (Espana) as well as *its* possible application in other European subsidiaries. *These* are our tentative conclusions.

1 _____

2 _____

– Although the number of Spanish respondents was low (see appendix ii) *this* did not invalidate the table from our point of view.

3 _____

– Bearing in mind the high percentage of Spanish respondents wishing to maintain a programme, *those* wishing to abandon should not be over-emphasized.

4 _____

– In Spain our workforce would be in favour of a flexitime programme, the introduction of *which* would lead to a measure of greater job satisfaction and thus higher productivity.

5 _____

– Opposition to the scheme is unlikely to come from the union representatives, *who* have little to gain by. . .

6 _____

A Answer these questions about the text.

1 What can you find in appendix ii?

2 Why should we pay attention to the percentage of Spanish respondents who wish to keep a programme?

3 What is felt would be the result of the introduction of the flexitime programme in Spain?

4 What was the objective of the London meeting?

B Say what the words in *italics* refer to.

Check your answers in the key.

Focus on Language 2

Before Llinares received any response from his report to the US he discussed it with Bob Wilde, an American working for Voltomatico in Mexico.

Listen to the cassette and say what the words in italics refer to.

REFERENCE WORD	REFERS TO
1 ...to introduce *it* here...	_____
2 ...but don't *they* run...	_____
3 ...No, *that's* the point...	_____
4 ...*they* don't and neither...	_____
5 ...encouraging, are *they?*	_____
6 ...you look at *them.*	_____
7 ...to drop *it,* which...	_____
8 ...it, *which* goes to...	_____
9 ...against *this,* are you?	_____
10 ...do think that *they* show...	_____

PRACTICE 3

Here are three passages which can be improved with the use of reference words.

Rewrite them, using the reference words given.

he (x 2)   which   they

a The Chancellor said yesterday that the Chancellor expected the cut in the basic rate of income tax to be reflected in lower pay settlements. The cut was announced on Tuesday. The Chancellor said that rapid growth in unit labour costs is keeping interest rates higher than the interest rates should be.

which   its

b Barcham, the pharmaceuticals and consumer products group, is selling off two of Barcham's businesses as part of Barcham's strategic group review. Barcham saw a change in its board of directors last year.

they (x 2)

c The Chancellor described oil companies as 'silly' when the oil companies threatened to pass on the increased tax on oil to motorists. "I think that it is pretty clear, after what has happened in the oil market and the degree of competition at the pumps, that if the oil companies are to put up prices the prices will come down again."

Check your answers in the key.

6

Forecasting

PART 1

**Language
Summary**

Some ways of expressing probability and certainty are given here.

Certainty
*Salaries will **definitely** rise.*
***I am sure** that sales will improve.*
*Sales are **bound to** go up by 15 percent.*
*We know that it **certainly** won't happen.*

Probability
*Our orders will **probably** be delivered in 72 hours.*
*With this system, rejects **should** go down by ten percent. The situation is **likely** to continue.*
*The **likelihood** is that the companies won't merge.*

Possibility
*If we don't cut costs, profits **could** drop.*
*It's **possible** we'll get the contract. I don't know.*
*Conditions **may** improve next year.*
*There **might** be trouble with the trade unions.*
*There's just a **chance** that profits will be better.*

Improbability
*The rate of 1:4 is **unlikely** to change.*
***I doubt if** the project will cost less than £50,000.*

**Listening for
information 1**

A company intends to install a new computerized order processing unit in six months time. Opinions are divided as to its eventual usefulness.

The order of the speakers is as follows:
Peter Barker   Sales Manager
Michael Hedges Accounts Manager
Jane Hobbs   Marketing Manager
John Taylor   Managing Director

Listen to the cassette and say if the following statements are *true* or *false*.

1 Peter Barker is certain that sales will improve.

2 Michael Hedges is just as certain as Peter Barker that the computerized order processing unit will benefit the company.

3 Jane Hobbs says she is 95 percent certain orders will be faster.

4 John Taylor feels there is a strong probability that the new system will cost too much.

> Check your
> answers in the key.

Focus on Language 1

Now listen again to the conversation and note the following in the grid below:

● the category of their forecasts *(certainly, probability, possibility)*;
● the forecasting language used;
● any figures given.

Speaker	Category of forecast	Words/Phases	Figures
Peter Barker			
Michael Hedges			
Jane Hobbs			
John Taylor			

Check your answers in the key.

Comprehension 1

Read the following text, written in 1991 and then say whether the statements are *true* or *false*.

The Future for European cars

By 1995, people throughout the world will be buying more than 55 million new cars a year, some 20% more than now – according to a major forecasting group. That is not as good news as it might seem for European car makers, who are likely to find themselves cash-strapped and losing market share.

After two glum years which culminated in a low point of 42 million sales last year, world registrations look likely to increase by 5% next year. It is expected that they will grow by 5% in 1992, 8% in 1993 and then settle down to an annual growth of 3–4% until 1995. The recovery is patchy though. Three quarters of next year's increase is likely to be accounted for by extra sales to the booming American market.

However, if the North American boom slows down in the mid-1990s, as is likely, then the future sales of European cars could well fall alarmingly. Finding new markets in the Far East or in the possibly expanding Eastern European market may then become a vital strategy for European car producers. This will certainly be so if the Japanese car makers continue to take market share within Europe itself from the European producers.

1 Car sales will go up by 20% in 1995.
2 It's probable that European car makers will lose market share.
3 Up to 1995, the best year for sales growth is expected to be 1994.
4 American sales may drop in the mid-1990s.
5 European car producers are unlikely to need to find new markets.

Check your answers in the key.

**Focus on
Language 2**

Now pick out the forecast words or phrases from the passage and say how certain the writer feels about the forecast by writing the words *possible   probable   certain* after each one.

Check your
answers in the key.

 **Listening for
information 2**

Listen to the three short dialogues and say which of the following statements are correct.

Dialogue A
Catherine and John are talking about Britain's inflation rate.

1 Catherine thinks the rate is certain to increase.

2 Catherine thinks oil prices will definitely increase.

3 Catherine thinks the increase in inflation will be great.

Dialogue B
Maureen is talking about the possibility of a woman becoming the next Italian president. She thinks

1 it's improbable that a woman could be the next Italian president.

2 it's impossible that a woman could be the next Italian president.

3 it's possible because it would add something new to the Italian political scene.

Dialogue C
Two managers, John Darby and Gill Evans, are discussing the benefit of a training course for a rather younger manager, Martin. In their opinion

1 Martin might benefit from the course.

2 Martin will definitely benefit.

3 Martin is likely to benefit.

Check your
answers in the key.

 **Focus on
Language 3**

Now listen to the three dialogues again, and answer the following questions.

1 In which dialogue is there a degree of possibility?

2 In which dialogue is there a strong degree of certainty?

3 In which dialogue is there a question about probability?

Check your
answers in the key.

PRACTICE 1 Here are two incomplete texts. Text A comes from a brief report on an airline. Text B comes from a report on a bank.

Read the texts and complete them, using the words or phrases in the left hand column.

Text A

The longer-term prospects of an airline are hard to assess since it is difficult to forecast the political and economic conditions. Owing to growing protectionism, it is safe to say that landing rights will be increasingly difficult to obtain. For this reason and in view of the existing surplus capacity in international air travel, the keen competition and price pressure is likely to **1** _____ with costs **2** _____ to rise. There is little likelihood of Swissair escaping these **3** _____ . But thanks to its modern aircraft fleet and solid financial base, the company commands an excellent market position. Given reasonably favourable conditions, the outlook is **4** _____ .

1 *go down*
   persist
   fall

2 *continuing*
   stopping
   needing

3 *costs*
   pressures
   influences

4 *gloomy*
   bright
   average

Text B

The greater risks encountered both at home and abroad in lending operations will, however, again necessitate appropriate allocations to provisions. **5** _____ , a good net result can be expected once again next year. Over the long term, the broad earnings base consisting of income from interest, commissions, securities and foreign exchange and precious metals trading constitutes a sound prerequisite for continued **6** _____ .

5 *In the same way*
   Nevertheless
   As a result

6 *growth*
   risk
   allocations

Check your answers in the key.

PRACTICE 2 You are an employee of a Swedish pharmaceutical company and you are due to make a short presentation about prospects for the coming year. You have information about performance so far in the three areas in the graphs below.

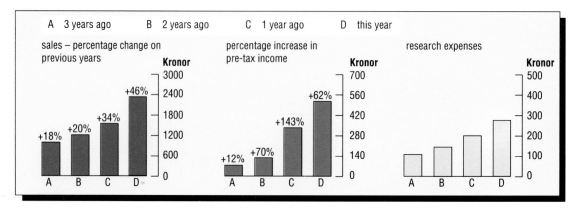

You also have information in the notes below about prospects for the coming year.

Use the notes to prepare a short presentation which will be based on the graphs. In your presentation refer to each graph in turn. Remember to 'signal' the introduction, change of topic and conclusion.

> NOTES   NEXT YEAR'S FORECASTS
>
> Sales: Sales about 2800m Swedish kronor — Strong probability
>
> Income: Income just over 700m Swedish kronor — Possibility
>
> Research: Expenses at about 400m Swedish kronor — Certainty

> Compare your presentation with the model in the key.

PART 2

Background

Wessex Information had a difficult time last year. After a few big surveys, such as those for Voltomatico and Vinoitalia, they had many enquiries but few clients actually asked for their services.

 **Listening for information 3**

One morning after a visit to their accountant, Jim Craig and a colleague, Mary Rogers, met to discuss the provisional end-of-year accounts.

Say if these statements are *true* or *false*.

1 Jim Craig feels there should be a better success rate on their business trips.

2 Mary Rogers has the possibility of a deal abroad.

3 Jim Craig is more pessimistic at the end of the conversation than at the beginning.

4 Mary Rogers is more optimistic than Jim Craig.

> Check your answers in the key.

Focus on Language 4

Complete the following extracts from Craig and Rogers' conversation.

1 There are _____ _____ _____ some jobs you just. . .

2 . . .I've got a contact that _____ _____ _____ lead to something.

3 . . .I've got a couple of things that _____ turn out okay.

4 . . .the Bordeaux deal _____ go ahead.

> Check your answers in the key.

Comprehension 2   That afternoon Jim Craig, Mary Rogers and another colleague, Ray Johnson, met to discuss future business and, in particular, a letter from Mr I L Talford of Karlston Furniture, one of the country's largest furniture companies.

Read the extract from the letter and answer the questions.

> . . . and as a well-known manufacturer of furniture for the British market, we are naturally interested in expanding our activities and promoting European and North American sales. However, to do this in the present economic climate without sufficient guarantees and a competent market survey would be inadvisable. Therefore we would be pleased to meet one of . . .

1   Is Karlston already selling into Europe?

2   When the writer says *to do this* what does he mean?

3   When the writer says *one of* who is he referring to?

> Check your answers in the key.

Listening for information 4   Jim Craig, Mary Rogers and Ray Johnson discuss Talford's letter.

1   What is Karlston's British market share: 15% or 50%?

2   Does Ray think this percentage could be improved?

3   Does Jim think it's certain they'll break into the European market?

4   Does Mary agree with Jim?

5   Does Ray feel Jim might be right or is definitely right?

Focus on Language 5   The following statements occur in the dialogue. Which of the alternatives (a, b, c) corresponds best to each?

1   . . .*it couldn't get any more if it tried.*

    a it might get more if. . .

    b it would be impossible to get more if. . .

    c it may not get more if. . .

2   . . .*they're bound to need a decent survey*. . .

    a they might need. . .

    b they will need. . .

    c they should need. . .

3   . . .*it's unlikely they'd be able to break into*. .

    a they probably wouldn't be able to. . .

    b they shouldn't be able to. . .

    c they may not be able to. . .

4   *I doubt if they'd have a chance.*

    a They don't have. . .

    b They have. . .

    c I don't think they have. . .

5   . . .*you could be right*. . .

    a you may be right. . .

    b I think you're right. . .

    c you're right. . .

> Check your answers in the key.

PRACTICE 3   Wessex Information then sent the following letter in reply.

Read the letter and complete it, using some of these phrases.

might be able to   may   will   certain that   likely that
unlikely that   bound to   might   could

Dear Mr Talford

Thank you very much for your letter in which you mentioned your plan to expand your business.

We would be very happy to meet you to discuss how we might be able to help. We would also be very happy to conduct a survey and we are _____(1) that, in these circumstances, a thorough investigation into the market is necessary. At this point in time it does seem that we _____(2) conduct a survey quite quickly.

It is quite _____(3) a preliminary survey would give us all the necessary information, although this _____(4) need to be backed up by some supplementary surveys later.

Yours faithfully

Check your answers in the key.

PRACTICE 4   At the beginning of the following week, which is October 7th, Mary Rogers sends a memo to Jim Craig, in which she mentions a problem that has just come up.

Use the notes below and the guides on the right of it to complete the memo.

To: Jim Craig
From: Mary Rogers
Date: October 7th
Reference: letter / to / Talford

problem about survey
just received telex from Bordeaux
want her to start next week
job / last six-eight weeks   probability
Ray / hear something about job in
   Newcastle   possibility
job / start in early November   possibility
last at least a month   probability
What do you suggest?   possibility

Compare your version with the model in the key.

7

Cause, effect and purpose

Aims   This unit focuses on those phrases and words which are used to express cause, effect and purpose. Some of these you will find immediately below and others you will meet later on in the unit.

Language Summary

The diagram below shows a situation fairly common to many developed countries.

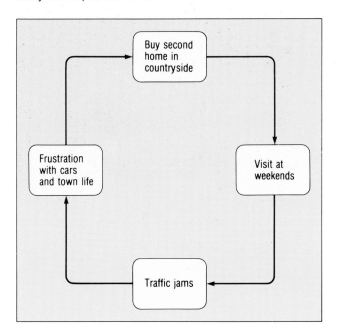

Read the following passage which describes the *vicious circle* shown above.

Many town-dwellers buy weekend homes *so that* they can spend peaceful weekends in the country. However, this *results in* huge traffic jams leaving the large metropolitan areas every Friday evening. *This means that* there is a lot of frustration on the roads and that, coupled with a general dissatisfaction at living in towns, *leads* people to buy weekend homes *in order to* find peace, but. . .

THE WORDS AND PHRASES IN ITALICS SIGNIFY:

Purpose

Cause
Effect

Cause
Purpose

Notice these other cause and effect signals.

- *Since* the company wasn't making profits, it was unable to invest in new machinery.

- The product didn't sell well *as* there was not enough money spent on marketing it.

- Prices rose *as a result of* the increase in oil prices.

- *Due to* the excellent labour relationships there were no strikes.

- Exports fell *owing to the fact* that the US economy was doing badly.

- The company became very competitive *because of* the great concentration on research and development.

Listening for information 1

J M Barnett is a company which produces sports goods and which has recently broken into the international market. It does not have a lot of free capital, but it has decided to invest in a weekend cottage for the use of its employees and guests from overseas.

Listen to the conversation between the two directors, Bob Mitchell and Karen Saunders, and answer the questions below.

1 Who seems more cautious about the idea, Bob Mitchell or Karen Saunders?

2 Is the cottage in the middle of the country or near the sea?

3 What kind of roofs can you commonly find in Wales?

4 What effect has the weather had?

5 Why is it so cheap?

> Check your answers in the key.

Focus on Language 1

Listen to the conversation again and complete the following extracts.

1 And of course, _____ it's in Wales, it's got a . . .

2 Well, it is a bit run down _____ _____ the . . .

3 But that _____ it's cheap.

4 Only £35,000 _____ _____ the work that's got to be done.

5 . . . it's a good investment. _____ it's only a few hours drive away . . .

> Check your answers in the key.

PRACTICE 1 A couple of years ago, the manufacturers of *Countryman* soap realized that their product had not been selling well. The marketing manager of the company said this was due to bad packaging while the production manager blamed poor distribution. The advertising manager said it was a consequence of unclear marketing objectives. However, they all agreed that something had to be done to rectify the situation.

Below is part of a report from the marketing manager on the current situation with the product. Read it and

a underline all signals of cause and effect.

b complete the graph.

> Countryman's initial success was due to our vigorous TV and Press promotion. This raised sales to 30,000 bars by the beginning of June. This rise continued till September when Samson came onto the market. By October our sales had levelled off at just over 100,000 units a month, and remained fairly static until December. At the time the colour of Countryman was changed from Apple Green to Azure Blue. As a result, sales went up steadily and by March of Year Two were around the 120,000 mark. After that, we started selling widely through supermarkets, having decided that Countryman could become a more down-market product. Owing to our supermarket outlets, sales rose to about 150,000 by June of Year Two. However, by October of Year Two distribution costs were rising fast and to offset this rise the price of Countryman was increased. This led to a slump in sales, which we are now experiencing – no more than 100,000 bars a month.

5

10

15

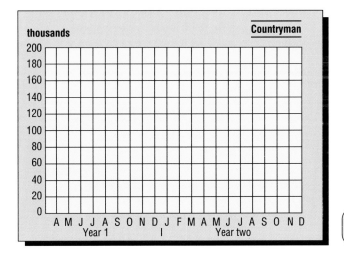

Check your answers in the key.

PRACTICE 2   *Countryman* was not abandoned and sales rose
dramatically after a well-conducted TV advertising
campaign.

On the strength of this, the manufacturers decided to
launch *Countrywoman* a year later. It was not a success.

Make a presentation showing why *Countrywoman* should
be abandoned. Use the information in the graph and in the
handwritten notes.

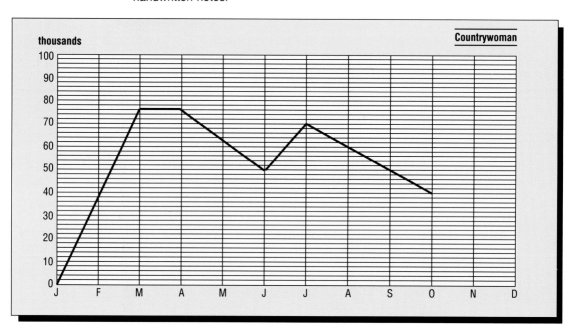

YEAR THREE

JAN – launch, regional radio advertising
FEB – sponsorship of women's sports events
MAR – advertising in up-market journals,
      sales outlets in beauty shops,
APR – Ash Grove, a competitor's soap,
      launched (20% cheaper)
MAY – Ash Grove in supermarkets
JUNE – COUNTRYWOMAN in supermarkets
JULY – company computerizes stock
      distribution
AUG – new packaging, 4 bars at 15% discount
SEP – regional distribution problems
OCT – withdrawn from market

Compare your
version with the
model in the key.

PART 2

Background

Plaisir de la Mer is a French pleasure boat manufacturing company based near Honfleur. Michelle Bernardon, the Managing Director, took over from her father only three years ago. The Bernardon family have been in the boat building business for three generations and have a high reputation for quality in the middle-range craft (five to seven metres in length).

Feeling that the market in France was beginning to saturate, Michelle Bernardon started to consider exporting to the UK. She made a few enquiries which were not encouraging. Most French boat building companies had had disappointing results in the UK market.

Nevertheless, she decided to have a survey carried out and contacted Mary Rogers at Wessex Information, as the company had been recommended by a friend.

After negotiations an agreement was made between Plaisir de la Mer and Wessex Information for the latter to carry out a survey of visitors to the London Boat Show which was to take place a few weeks later.

Listening for information 2

Listen to this interview which takes place at the Boat Show and answer the questions.

1   Does the interviewee have a boat at present?

2   What sort of price does he wish to pay?

3   Give one reason mentioned by the interviewee for owning a boat.

4   How far away from the coast does he live?

5   Is he likely to buy a French boat?

> Check your answers in the key.

Focus on Language 2

Listen to the interview again and complete the following extracts.

1 . . .something around five or six metres probably, _____ I'm limited by price.

2 . . .it's for use at weekends, _____ _____ my kids can get used to. . .

3 Well, it _____ _____ being able to sail every weekend. . .

4 . . .about ten percent higher for an equivalent craft _____ _____ the costs of exporting. . .

> Check your answers in the key.

Listening for information 3

Eventually *Plaisir de la Mer* decided to go ahead with exporting to the UK. Wessex Information took on a liasion role, with Mary Rogers acting as occasional advisor.

It is now January of year two. The company's first year has been a qualified success and Michelle Bernardon is looking forward to a profitable second year, especially with the annual Boat Show coming up soon. However, there is trouble ahead.

One day Michelle Bernardon phones Mary Rogers with some bad news. Listen to the conversation and answer the following questions.

1 What is the problem with Peterson and Roberts?

2 Is Michelle pleased with the number of category ones sold in the UK?

3 Does Mary Rogers say what would happen if Michelle loses credibility?

4 Why might Michelle want to find another company?

5 Finding this company might be rather expensive. What does Mary Rogers say that tells you this?

6 What is Mary Roger's final recommendation?

> Check your answers in the key.

Focus on Language 3

Listen to the conversation again and complete the following extracts.

1 . . .deliver on time for the London Boat Show. That _____ I must cancel our stand.

2 . . .you'll lose credibility and you know what that _____ _____ _____ .

3 Yes, but look. _____ _____ _____ get *The Cutter* to the Boat Show we'd have to. . .

4 At least _____ _____ _____ _____ you wouldn't be forgotten on the UK market. . .

> Check your answers in the key.

PRACTICE 3   What would you do in Michelle Bernardon's position?

Bear in mind:

EFFECTS

- the dangers of subcontracting work to possibly unknown companies

delivery problems

- the effects of not exhibiting at the London Boat Show

lose credibility

- poor sales of present lines

prices too high

- the cost factor

lost deposit

Write out a short report, using cause, effect and purpose signals, the notes given above, and the guide below.

We're thinking of cancelling

_____

_____

However, not exhibiting at the Boat Show _____

_____

On the other hand, _____

_____

Compare your version with the model in the key.

Key: Tapescript and answers

UNIT 1 TAPESCRIPT AND ANSWERS

Listening for information 1

a seventeen (17)
b two hundred and thirteen (213)
c three hundred and thirty-three (333)
d fifty (50)
e two hundred and eighteen (218)
f ninety thousand (90,000)
g six thousand (6,000)
h thirty thousand (30,000)
i thirty (30)
j six thousand three hundred and sixteen (6,316)

PRACTICE 1

a four hundred and ninety-eight million, four hundred and fourteen thousand
b ten million, forty-one thousand
c fifty-five million, nine hundred and seventy-two thousand
d three million, five hundred and twenty-two thousand
e fifty-seven million, five hundred and thirty-one thousand

Listening for information 2

In 1991 the population of Belgium was 2.9% of the total European Community, and the now unified Germany's was 22.9%. France had a lower population of 16.3%, and Ireland's was quite small – only 1%. Britain's population was similar to that of France – 16.7%.

PRACTICE 2

a ninety-five divided by six
b seventeen times eighteen
c eighty-six minus seventeen
d twelve plus three hundred and forty-six
e P is less/smaller than Q
f K is more/greater than G

Listening for information 3

1 Last year our turnover went up by nearly *a quarter*, to £70,000, and, if we take away the cost of renting premises. . .

2 Only a few more kilometres and we're nearly *two thirds* of the way home.

3 If you computerized the pay section, you could divide at least *50%* of the work with the accounts department.

4 Look, by car the journey's going to take two hours. It'll take me *three times that* by train, the connections are so bad.

5 Something must be wrong. Nearly *a quarter* of our petty cash goes in photocopying and, if we add the salesmen's restaurant bills, there's nothing left for stamps.

Focus on Language

The unemployment situation for men in the USA steadily improved between 1982 and 1989. In 1982 the rate of unemployment stood at *almost five* percent, but fell to *just over four* percent in 1984. By 1989 it was *getting on* for *two percent* but began to rise around that time. By 1991 the figure stood at *approximately three and a half* percent.

The unemployment rate for USA men was well below that shown for European men during this period. In fact it was *roughly two percent lower* in 1991.

PRACTICE 3

Model version

In 1982, the unemployment rate for men in Europe stood at just over five percent of the Labour Force. By 1991 it was still approximately five percent, having been roughly stable throughout the period. Nevertheless, the unemployment rate for European men can be seen to be well over that recorded for USA men, almost three percent higher in the period 1988 to 1990.

Listening for information 4

Although this motor rotates only 43 rpm, it's an extremely efficient machine which consumes only 35 kilowatts per hour giving it an input/efficiency rate of one to nine. At £99.50, it's a very good bargain, especially as its depreciation has been calculated at only eight percent per year. It can of course be hired but this is rather expensive – £27 a month. However, we must remember that hiring does have . . .

RATE OF MOTOR	*43 rpm*
POWER CONSUMPTION	*35 kw per hour*
EFFICIENCY RATE	*1 : 9*
PRICE	*£99.50*
ANNUAL DEPRECIATION	*8%*
HIRE CHARGE	*£27 per month*

UNIT 2   TAPESCRIPT AND ANSWERS

Focus on Language 1

(1) *I'd like to talk about* the comparative figures for steel production in the EC, USA and Japan in the years 1972 and 1991.

(2) *As you can see from the graph*, production fell sharply in the EC and the States, but rose in Japan during this period. The fall in Europe was from just under 140 to roughly 100 million tonnes, and in the USA from 123 million tonnes to just over 90.

(3) *If we look at the figures for* Japan, the rise is considerable – from 97 million tonnes to almost 110.

PRACTICE 1

INTRODUCING A SUBJECT	SEQUENCING	REFERRING TO TEXT/VISUALS	CHANGING A TOPIC	CONCLUDING
g i j	b h l	c m	d e	a f k

PRACTICE 2   Model version

This morning I'm going to talk briefly about consumer price changes in five major countries during the period 1988 to 1991.

Let's look at the United States figures. As you can see, the annual change in consumer prices rose from around 4% in 1988 to just under 6% in 1990, before falling back to around 3% in 1991. Throughout this period, the United States had the second highest rate of inflation of the five countries considered.

Now, turning to France, we can see that consumer prices rose less quickly than those in Britain and the United States throughout this period. Inflation rose to over 3% in 1989 and 1990, before falling back to just over 2% in 1991. Indeed by 1991, the inflation rate in France had fallen below that in Germany and was now equal to that in Japan.

PART 2

Comprehension Check

Craig receives a telephone call . . .

Craig   Wessex Information. Can I help you?

Callaghan   May I speak to Jimmy Craig please?

Craig   Speaking.

Callaghan   This is Stewart Callaghan, of Coles. You've probably never heard of us but we manufacture anti-personnel devices for domestic use.

Craig   Sorry?

Callaghan   We sell portable gas sprays that can be used in case of assault or robbery.

Craig   Oh, I see. Where do you sell?

Callaghan   In quite a few of the EC countries, but we want to expand – maybe to Scandinavia or the Middle East, for example.

Craig   Uh-huh, and how do you think I can help you?

Callaghan   I've read an article about your company in a magazine and, well, I was interested in your approach. You see, we're still fairly small and we haven't got any agents in . . .well, Scandinavia, for example, so I wondered if you might have any contacts there.

Craig   Well, I may be able to help you. In fact I do know some people. What do you want exactly?

Callaghan   What I'd really like is crime statistics broken down for each Scandinavian country.

1 False   **2** True   **3** False   **4** True   **5** True

Listening for information 1

Craig's presentation. . .

I'm going to speak to you about the rates of assault in the Nordic countries. I've chosen this particular crime as it's the one where Cole's product could be most useful. The second part of my presentation will be about market prospects for Coles.

Right, I'll deal with each country in turn, so let's start with Sweden as it's the largest country and its crime profile is perhaps the most representative.

If we look at this transparency on the OHP, we can see that the number of assaults went up between 1950 and 1988 – in fact from just over 7,000 in 1950 – 7,359 to be exact – to 27,825 in 1988. In other words, by 1988 there were almost 500 assaults per 100,000 inhabitants.

Let's first look at the period 1950 to 1960. Until around 1960 there were in the region of eight to nine thousand assaults per year. Then, turning to the next decade, we notice that by 1970 things had worsened. The figure of 18,385 was slightly more than double that of 1960 . . .

Year	Number of assaults	Number of assaults per 100,000 inhabitants aged 15 or over
1950	7,359	
1970	18,385	
1988	27,825	491

Focus on Language 2

1 I'm *going to speak to you about* the rates of assault in the Nordic countries. . .

2 *If we look at this* transparency on the OHP, we can see. . .

3 *Let's first look at* the period 1950 to 1960.

Listening for information 2

Craig continues his presentation. . .

We'll be looking at Finland in terms of assaults per 100,000 inhabitants.

We can see that assault offences more than doubled during the period in question – from 226 per hundred thousand in 1950 to getting on for 480 in 1988, But, again, the rise wasn't continuous. If we take the years in ten year blocks, we can see that assaults actually went down in 1960 to just under 200, but then rose to 355 in 1970. Now, if I can draw your attention to the period 1971 to 1975, you can see that it is marked by a rise to about 400 in '75 followed by a fall to approximately 350 in 1977–78, But by 1979, the assault rate was at 402 per hundred thousand and went up to 434 in 1981 rising steadily to 478 in 1988. I'd now like to refer back to the Swedish situation. . .

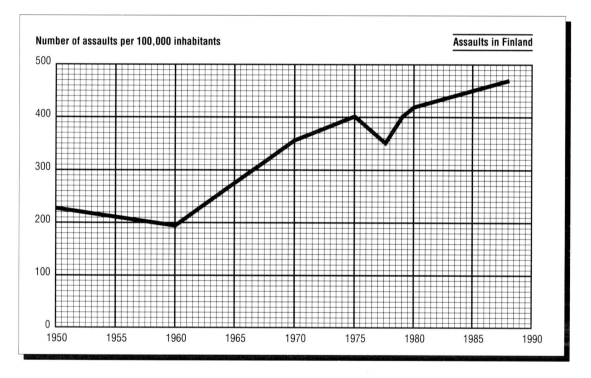

Focus on Language 3

1 *We'll be looking at* Finland *in terms of* assaults per. . .

2 *Now, if I can draw* your attention to. . .

3 *I'd now like to refer back to* the Swedish. . .

4 *If I can go back to. . .*

and

Now I'd like to return to. . .

PRACTICE 3　Model version

I'd like to give you a short outline of my career development up till now.

When I finished my education in 1964, I joined a textile company in the north as a salesman, and I worked there for about two years. However, as you know the textile industry has gone through a bad time in Europe, and Britain isn't the only European country where markets have disappeared. In fact, I could see the sort of problem we were going to get from the Far Eastern markets very early on.

Anyway, to come back to what happened next. I left Tompsons, the textile company, and joined Roberts. I've prepared a diagram to show you more clearly the development over the next few years. So, this is it. As you can see, in 1967 I joined Roberts, again as a salesman. Roberts is a multi-product food processing company, and, to begin with, I worked exclusively in the dairy sector here. There were six of us. And that's me. One of the six salesman. Then, in 1969, the head of that sales division left and I was asked to take his place, which I did. If I could just go back to that point about finishing my education. Of course, that's not strictly true. Over the years I've attended a great many training courses, in sales, and, of course, marketing.

Then we come to 1973, when I moved across to marketing. This was a big step for me. Roberts sent me to Michigan for a year, and I then worked out in Singapore with our Far East headquarters until 1978. I was in charge there of market planning for the Far East. Good years, they were. In 1978 I came back, and became assistant marketing director UK. Bob Jones, my direct superior, retired in '82 and I took his place. Now, in the early 1990s, I am looking towards actively developing our food processing activities in Eastern Europe and the Soviet Republics. The problems they now face there in food distribution create a good market opportunity for us. It is this kind of strategic planning which is now my major contribution to the company.

So there you are. In many ways it's a fairly straightforward and logical path. No real surprises.

UNIT 3　TAPESCRIPT AND ANSWERS

Focus on Language 1

During the year the sales of the French motor car companies fell considerably. For example, Renault's market share dropped to about 11% and there was a similar decline in Citroen's share of the market. On the other hand, Ford and the big German manufacturers did well, with Ford's share rising to over 12%. Other companies with an increase in market share included Volvo and some of the Japanese companies.

1 fell **2** dropped **3** decline **4** rising **5** increase

Focus on Language 2

You probably know that Avonville's population is a *great deal higher* than Bathford's, but what surprises many people is that Abbotsbury's is only *slightly lower* than Tipworth's population. Tipworth's population is now *substantially higher* than ten years ago.

Focus on Language 3

There was a *rapid* increase in sales in the south-west of the country for product A last year, although in the north-east sales continued to decline *steadily*. This was not unexpected. Product B sales rose *sharply* if we take the country as a whole, but again in the north-east there continued to be a *gradual* decline.

Focus on Language 4

Like most other countries shown on the table, the overall trend was downward.

In 1972 there were 547,000 in West Germany, the highest figure of all the European countries. Then, over the next two years there was a sharp drop in the number of accidents, to slightly over 460,000 in 1974.

Following that, over the years 1974 to '77, the number of accidents rose a little each year, for example 523,000 in 1977. This figure remained the same in 1978.

Now, looking at the next year on the table, 1979, we can see that the number of accidents went down by 23,000, only to increase again in 1980 to 514,000. In 1981 the figure fell somewhat to 488,000, but this was still by far the highest number of accidents of any of the countries quoted for that year. By 1988, the number of accidents had fallen still further, to 448,000.

1 downward **2** sharp drop **3** rose a little
4 remained the same **5** went down by **6** increase
7 fell somewhat **8** had fallen still further

PRACTICE 1

Model version

I'm going to talk about the road accident figures in the UK. The total number of accidents fluctuated quite a lot during the period 1972–1988. If you look at the table you can see that in 1972 the figure was 360,000, while in 1988 it had fallen to 313,000, a drop of 47,000. The best year in the period 1972–78 was 1974 when it stood at 332,000, after which it rose to a new peak of slightly under 360,000 in 1978. We can see that from 1978–88 there was there a steady fall in the number of road accidents.

PRACTICE 2

Model version

The DBM bicycle was launched in 1985 and sales rose steadily over the following two year period, reaching a total of 40,000 units in 1987. Over the next 12 months sales fluctuated considerably, reaching a peak of around 50,000 units at the end of 1988. After that, the sales dropped dramatically, falling to just below 20,000 at the end of '89. A further drop was sustained over the following months, but after that the situation picked up and the sales increased quite sharply.

Comprehension 1 False 2 True 3 True 4 True 5 False 6 True
7 True 8 True

PART 2

Comprehension Check

Mary Rogers	Wessex Information. Can I help you?
Tom Johnson	Well, I hope so. My name's Tom Johnson. I'm the marketing manager of Vinoitalia-UK. You may have heard of us.
Mary Rogers	Yes, well, er, I . . .
Tom Johnson	Aperitifs, that sort of thing.
Mary Rogers	Oh yes, of course. How can I help you Mr Johnson?
Tom Johnson	Well, I want to know if you can help us get statistics on traffic accidents.
Mary Rogers	Well, certainly, but if you could give me some more details, then I can . . .
Tom Johnson	Well, we're the British subsidiary of an Italian company, Vinoitalia, you know, and we're thinking of developing some new lines for Britain, drinks for the British market.
Mary Rogers	But I don't see why you want information on traffic accidents.
Tom Johnson	Ok, I'll explain. We're planning to introduce a new range. . .

1 True 2 False 3 True 4 True

Listening for information

Mary Rogers' presentation to Vinoitalia

Good morning. The aim of my presentation today is to describe to you why I think that a grape-based but non-alcoholic aperitif will sell well in Britain and to get your agreement for Wessex Information to carry out a market survey in the UK on drinking patterns of young people. . .

. . . Now let's turn to the graph.

First, let's take the years 1980 to 1982. This period saw a rise in the number of fatal and serious injuries. But the rise was not regular. In 1981 the number of such injuries actually fell, from 71,000 in the previous year to 70,000, before rising again in 1982 to 72,000. Then came a considerable drop in 1983, from 72,000 fatal and serious injuries in the previous year to as few as 65,000 in 1983.

The second phase we'll look at spans the years 1983 to 1987. The number of fatal and serious road accident victims fell steadily in this period from 65,000 in 1983 to around 62,000 in 1986. The number then fell quite sharply in 1987 to around 59,000.

Finally, let us look at the period 1987 to 1990. During this time there was a steady fall in the number of fatal and serious road accident victims from 59,000 in 1987 to around 57,000 in 1989, with a sharper fall in 1990 to as few as 55,000 victims.

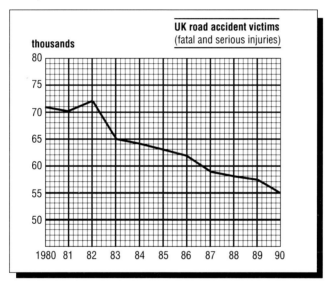

UK road accident victims (fatal and serious injuries)

PRACTICE 3 **Suggested answers**

1 increased/rose   **2** continued   **3** 40,000   **4** lower
5 rise/peak   **6** fall   **7** peak   **8** 55,000

PRACTICE 4   **a** Fig 4   **c** Fig 6   **e** Fig 5
             b fig 3   **d** Fig 2   **f** Fig 1

PRACTICE 5   **1** There was a rise in production of six percent.

             2 There is a steady increase in consumption in Spain.

             3 There was a dramatic fall in sales from 200,000 to 60,000 in one year.

             4 There will probably be considerable fluctuation this year.

             5 There were steady increases in production in 1989.

             6 There has been substantial growth in the market over the past two years.

PRACTICE 6   Model version

The 2B3 was launched in 1986, and by 1987 sales had risen to just under 10,000. After that, sales rose quite sharply. At the end of 1987 they peaked momentarily at 30,000, before dropping slightly at the beginning of 1988. However, afterwards they picked up again and rose quite spectacularly until levelling out at about 55,000 at the end of 1989.

UNIT 4 TAPESCRIPT AND ANSWERS

Listening for information 1

A Well, those were the basic trends. Now, do you have any questions?

B Yes. What about the situation in Italy?

A The Italian ratio was slightly lower than the Common Market average of about 1,000 beds per 100,000 people.

C And how about Northern Europe, the Netherlands, for example?

A Well, the Dutch ratio of slightly over 1,200 beds per 100,000 was far higher than the average in 1988, while Sweden had the largest number of beds available. The figure there was over 1,400 – very high compared with Denmark where it was only 680.

C I'm rather surprised about the States. Do you know why the ratio is so low?

A A good question. Many of you may be surprised to know that you'll find a hospital bed much more easily in the majority of the Common Market countries than in the USA, where the ratio of beds was considerably lower than the Common Market average in the region of 600 beds per 100,000.

1 Sweden   2 The Netherlands   3 Italy   4 USA

Focus on Language 1

1 lower than   2 far higher than   3 lower than

Focus on Language 2

Of course, we can only guess at the real reason why the situation in the States is a great deal worse than in a country like Sweden. There's far more government control of the hospital network in Scandinavia than in America, although it's surprising that the United Kingdom, where the government also has a strong control of the health service, has a much lower number of beds than a country like Germany.

1 great deal   2 far   3 much lower

PRACTICE 1   Model version

There is a great range in the numbers of doctors per 100,000 inhabitants in various parts of the world, as we can see from the chart. It is surprising that the figure for Italy should be a great deal higher than for the United Kingdom, but that is the case. In Italy the figure is around 400, while in the United Kingdom it is only a little over 160 doctors per 100,000 inhabitants. Both Spain and Belgium have considerably higher figures than the United Kingdom – slightly over 350 in Spain and about 310 in Belgium.

Listening for information 2

There are quite a few surprises when we look at the chart of the number of TVs per 100 inhabitants for the countries shown.

For example, although Denmark is a relatively small country, its ratio of 37 TV sets for every 100 inhabitants was higher than that for France.

And then, despite its reputation for technology, the ratio for Japan of 58 per 100 was substantially lower than that for the USA.

What's more, the numbers of channels available doesn't seem to have much effect on TV ownership. Italy had many more channels than Ireland; nevertheless, they both had a ratio of around 25 TVs per 100.

Most European countries had between 30 and 40 TVs per hundred, while, unsurprisingly, the USA was out in front with a ratio of over 80 TVs to every 100 inhabitants.

1 USA   **2** Japan   **3** Denmark   **4** Italy and Ireland

Focus on Language 3

1 although   **2** despite   **3** nevertheless   **4** while

PRACTICE 2   Model version

Compared to Japan and the European countries, the United States is well ahead when it comes to the number of cars per hundred inhabitants. The figure there is 60 for every 100 inhabitants, whereas in Japan it is only 29. The United Kingdom, despite its position as an industrial manufacturing country, also has a rather low figure of 41 cars for every 100 inhabitants.

Focus on Language 4

A And which country had the highest ratio of phones to people?

B Well, Sweden, but both Sweden and the USA had getting on for 90 per 100 inhabitants.

A And what about the Mediterranean countries? You see, I'm particularly interested in them.

B Well, let's see, the ratio for Spain was similar to Greece, around 35 per 100, while Portugal was around 20 per 100, rather like Ireland, in fact.

1 both   **2** similar to   **3** like

PRACTICE 3   Model version

If we look at the chart, we can see that both Germany and Britain have quite a high number of phones per 100 inhabitants, while in Spain it is quite a lot lower. Germany's figure was 63 per 100 inhabitants, the UK's 57, but in Spain it was only 36. However, neither Ireland nor Portugal reached even this figure. In Ireland the number of phones per 100 inhabitants was 23 and in Portugal it was 21.

PRACTICE 4   **1** while/although   **2** However   **3** similarly
4 In contrast   **5** although

PART 2

Comprehension   **1** True   **2** False   **3** False   **4** True   **5** True
6 False   **7** True

PRACTICE 5   **1** Whereas   **2** Compared to   **3** in contrast to
4 against

PRACTICE 6   Model version

Switzerland and the UK show both differences and similarities. Although both countries show strong similarities in the numbers of respondents who wish to try the programme in the next five years or enlarge the programme, in the UK the 45.6% figure for those who have tried flexitime is considerably lower than Switzerland's 68.5%, and indeed lower than all the other countries in the table. Likewise, when looking at percentages of respondents who had not tried or had no plans to try flexitime, one finds a similar correlation. Most significant of all, perhaps, is the enormous 14% of all UK companies who have dropped the programme or will drop it – a figure which neither Switzerland nor any of the other countries except Spain begins to approach.

UNIT 5   TAPESCRIPT AND ANSWERS

Focus on Language 1

Scott	I hear your company's just bought its own premises in Paris.
Werner	Yes, about a month ago. It was a big investment, but we think it will pay off.
Scott	What are they like?
Werner	Oh, nothing spectacular. Three adjoining offices in the third district.
Scott	Expensive?
Werner	Fairly, but you know, Scott, if you want a decent place which you can receive clients in, you've got to pay for it.
Scott	Yeah, you're right there.

1 Werner's company   **2** investment   **3** premises
4 place (meaning the premises)

PRACTICE 1

1 its   **2** that   **3** its   **4** whose   **5** that   **6** its   **7** these

Comprehension 1

A   **1** False   **2** True   **3** False   **4** False

B   **1** cliché   **2** senior executives   **3** someone
4 senior executives   **5** their partner's career
6 spouses   **7** other sacrifices   **8** the fact that the sacrifices are thought to be worthwhile

PRACTICE 2

1 each   **2** Both   **3** It   **4** who   **5** which   **6** This

PART 2

Comprehension 2

A

1   the number of Spanish respondents

2   because we shouldn't over-emphasize the percentage of respondents who do wish to abandon their programmes

3   it would lead to greater job satisfaction / productivity

4   to discuss the question of flexitime for Voltomatico

B

1 flexitime   **2** the four conclusions below
3 the low number of Spanish respondents
4 the Spanish respondents   **5** flexitime programme
6 union representatives

Focus on Language 2

Llinares	. . .so this morning I want to put you in the picture about Voltomatico's position on flexitime. If we really want to introduce *it* here, we must show a common front to our American colleagues.
Bob Wilde	But don't *they* run a scheme?
Llinares	No, *that's* the whole point – *they* don't and neither do any of the other European subsidiaries for that matter. Right, let's look at these figures on the OHP.
Bob Wilde	Not very encouraging, are *they*?
Llinares	It depends how you look at *them*. On the one hand, we've got Spain with a fairly low number of companies who've actually tried flexitime, and, on the other hand, only 9% actually want to drop *it, which* goes to prove that we haven't been very adventurous here.
Bob Wilde	Look Garcia, can I say something? It seems that you want to convince the Americans that a statistic based on only 70 Spanish companies is enough to make a major policy change.
Llinares	You're not against *this,* are you?
Bob Wilde	Of course not. I'm trying to be practical, from their viewpoint.
Llinares	I agree that these statistics aren't enough on their own, but I do think that *they* show there is room for. . .

1 flexitime 2 American colleagues
3 the fact that they don't run a scheme
4 American colleagues 5 figures 6 figures
7 flexitime 8 the fact that only 9% want to drop it
9 introducing flexitime 10 statistics

PRACTICE 3 Model versions

a The Chancellor said yesterday that *he* expected the cut in the basic rate of income tax, *which* was announced on Tuesday, to be reflected in lower pay settlements. *He* said that rapid growth in unit labour costs is keeping interest rates higher than *they* should be.

b Barcham, the pharmaceuticals and consumer products group *which* saw a change in its board of directors last year, is selling off two of *its* businesses as part of its strategic group review.

c The Chancellor described oil companies as 'silly' when *they* threatened to pass on the increased tax on oil to motorists. "I think that it is pretty clear, after what has happened in the oil market and the degree of competition at the pumps, that if the oil companies are to put up prices *they* will come down again."

UNIT 6 TAPESCRIPTS AND ANSWERS

Listening for information 1

Peter Barker I'm sure that this new system'll mean real benefits for the sales force. I mean, it's bound to push sales up by at least 20%, because the orders'll be processed faster and we won't have to keep on telling our customers. . .

Michael Hedges Look, it could be just what we need – an order processing system that might cut out 80% of our admin. paperwork. And it could – if properly handled – lower delivery times by an average of three days, and that would be beneficial to. . .

Jane Hobbs Logically, this procedure should speed up order processing. It's likely that 95% of our orders will be at delivery point on time and that's obviously. . .

John Taylor I doubt if this new system will help much. Bearing in mind our transport and distribution problems, I don't think we'll be able to deliver any faster. Anyway, the cost of this adventure's unlikely to be less than £250,000 so obviously I'm rather sceptical.

1 True **2** False **3** False **4** True

Focus on Language 1

Speaker	Category of forecast	Words/Phrases	Figures
Peter Barker	certainty	*it's bound to*	20%
Michael Hedges	possibility	*could / might*	80%
Jane Hobbs	probability	*should / likely that*	95%
John Taylor	(im)probability	*unlikely to be*	£250,000

Comprehension 1

1 False **2** True **3** False **4** True **5** False

Focus on Language 2

will be buying (line 2)	certain
might seem (line 6)	possible
likely to find (line 7)	probable
look likely to increase (line 13)	probable
expected that they will grow (line 14)	probable
likely to be accounted for (line 20)	probable
as is likely (line 25)	probable
could well fall alarmingly (line 26)	probable
may then become (line 30)	possible
will certainly be so (line 31)	certain

Listening for information 2

Dialogue A

Catherine	Did you know that at the moment Britain's got one of the best inflation rates in Europe?
John	It's not bad, is it?
Catherine	Not even three percent, but I'm afraid it'll get slightly higher again. Bound to, really.
John	You think so?
Catherine	Well, when oil prices start going up again – and they will – inflation's bound to follow. Can't win, can you?

Dialogue B

Maureen	What are the chances then, Francesco? What do you think?
Francesco	What? Of an Italian woman president?
Maureen	Yes. Why not?
Francesco	Well, it's never happened before has it? And what about the men? How would they react?
Maureen	Ah, but the Italians are very innovative. I think the Italians like to see something new and, for that reason alone, I think there's a good chance.

Dialogue C

John Darby	Do you think Martin's likely to be a better manager?
Gill Evans	Yes. I mean, we're spending enough money on it.
John Darby	Well, I think he should understand how to run his department better. If that's not the case, we'll need to think again, but it's unlikely he won't gain from the experience.
Gill Evans	I agree.

Dialogue A 1 and 2   Dialogue B 3   Dialogue C 3

Focus on Language 3

1 Dialogue B   2 Dialogue A   3 Dialogue C

PRACTICE 1

1 persist   2 continuing   3 influences   4 bright
5 Nevertheless   6 growth

PRACTICE 2

Model version

I'd like to speak briefly about the future trends we can expect to see in our company, and to do that with particular reference to three graphs.

The first, here, shows sales. The trend so far has been pretty good and this has been a good year for us with an increase of 46%. I think that next year we will very likely have another major rise in sales to about 2,800 million kronor.

As far as the income is concerned, as you can see in this second graph, the trend has also been positive. I think we might reach a figure of just over 700 million in the coming year.

Finally, let's look at Research – a strong point with us. The figure is very high this year, and is going to be high next year too. About 400 million Swedish kronor, in fact.

PART 2

Listening for information 3

Jim Craig	I'm not really happy with the way things look, to tell you the truth. Look at column 401 – that's mainly hotels and travel. There's nearly 60 trips there and what did we get out of it? Six or seven jobs, that's all.
Mary Rogers	Oh, hold on, Jim. There are bound to be some jobs that you can't get.
Jim Craig	Yes, but not so many.
Mary Rogers	Okay, but I've got a contact that will most likely lead to something. I wanted to tell you about it...
Jim Craig	When can you expect to hear?
Mary Rogers	Well, it's the French deal. With Bordeaux.
Jim Craig	That one? Well, I suppose that's something. If it comes off. And I suppose I've got a couple of things that might turn out okay.
Mary Rogers	I really think the Bordeaux deal should go ahead. When can we talk?
Jim Craig	Well, how about tomorrow morning some time?

1 True **2** True **3** False **4** True

Focus on Language 4

1 bound to be **2** will most likely **3** might **4** should

Comprehension 2

1 No. **2** promote European and North American sales
3 the staff at Wessex Information

Listening for information 4

Ray	The point is, Karlston's got about 15% of the British furniture market, and it couldn't get anymore if it tried. So they've got to find markets abroad. So they're bound to need a decent survey, an international one to find out...

Jim	Hold on, Ray, it's unlikely they'd be able to break into the European market, anyway. Frankly, I think Talford's being far too optimistic. The British don't often sell furniture into Europe, let alone the States.
Mary	Frankly, I doubt they'd have a chance. Anyway, is this something we want to do, or not?
Ray	Well, you could be right, but we're not in business to say whether Karlston is right or not. We're here to sell him our services. So, let's give him what he wants.

1 15%   **2** No.   **3** No (he thinks it's unlikely).
4 Yes.   **5** Ray feels Jim might be right.

Focus on Language 5   1 b   2 b   3 a   4 c   5 a

PRACTICE 3   **1** certain that   **2** might be able to/could
3 likely that   **4** might

PRACTICE 4   Model version

> To: *Jim Craig*
> From: *Mary Rogers*
> Date: *October 7th*
> Reference: *Our letter to Mr Talford, Karlston*
>
> *With reference to our letter to Mr Talford at Karlston, I think we will (are going to) have a problem. I've just had a telex from Bordeaux, and they want me to start next week. I think the job could (might) last six to eight weeks. Also, I think Ray might (could, may) hear something new about a job in Newcastle which he thinks is likely to (could probably) start early November and could (might) last at least a month. What do you suggest?*

UNIT 7   TAPESCRIPT AND ANSWERS

Listening for information 1

Karen Saunders	I think it's a bargain, Bob.
Bob Mitchell	Hold on a minute. Where is it, first of all?
Karen Saunders	In Wales – a village near the coast.
Bob Mitchell	And what's it like?
Karen Saunders	There are three downstairs rooms, including the kitchen. And, of course, since it's in Wales, it's got a slate roof and. . .

Bob Mitchell	I mean structurally. Is it sound?
Karen Saunders	Well, it's a bit run down due to the weather, and, of course, it hasn't been lived in for 15 years.
Bob Mitchell	15 years!
Karen Saunders	But that means it's cheap.
Bob Mitchell	Must be a wreck. How much is it?
Karen Saunders	Only £35,000 – because of the work that's got to be done. Anyway, it's a good investment. As it's only a few hours' drive quite a lot of people will want to use it.

1 Bob Mitchell **2** near the sea **3** slate
4 the cottage is a bit run down **5** because of the work that's got to be done

Focus on Language 1

1 since **2** due to **3** means **4** because of **5** As

PRACTICE 1

a *due to* (lines 1–2)   *As a result* (lines 8–9)
Owing to (line 13)   *This led to* (line 17)

b

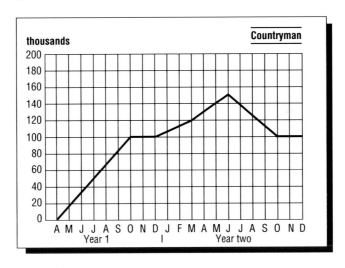

PRACTICE 2 Model version

The sales curve for Countrywoman shows a classic failure of a product to gain secure entry in the market. Without going into the details at the moment, very briefly this is what happened. The product was launched in January with widespread advertising on regional radio accompanying the main advertising in selected magazines. In February there was some sponsorship of women's sports events, especially athletics. By March, due to these activities, sales were running at 75,000 a month. At that time there was more advertising in up-market journals and at points of sale, but there was no increase in sales as a result of this effort. In fact, sales levelled off and started to fall in April. This may have been partly owing to the launch of Ash Grove, which was selling at 20% less than Countrywoman. Ash Grove was the first to gain acceptance in supermarkets, beating our product by one month, although our presence later in those outlets almost certainly led to a temporary rise in sales, up from just over 50,000 at the beginning of June to about 70,000 in July. The rest of the story is well known. We installed a new computerized stock system, introduced new packaging with four bars going at 15% discount, but these did not result in a rise in sales. In fact, we developed considerable regional distribution problems, and as Countrywoman was obviously continuing to lose ground to Ash Grove, we decided temporarily to withdraw the product from the market.

PART 2

Listening for information 2

A Excuse me, could I ask you a few questions? I'm doing a survey.

B Er, yes, okay.

A Do you own a boat at present?

B No, but I used to – before I had a family.

A Are you thinking of buying another one?

B Maybe, yes. But there's so much choice here.

A Yes, er. . .what length of craft are you thinking of?

B Well, something around five or six metres in probably, as I'm limited by price.

A And what is your price range?

B Oh, about four to five thousand. You see, it's only for use at weekends, so that my kids can get used to sailing when they're young.

A That's important for you, is it?

B Oh, yes, very.

A And how would owning a boat change your lifestyle?

B Well, it would mean being able to sail every weekend. The sea's only 25 miles from where we live.

A Right. What would your reactions be to buying a French boat?

B A French boat. Hmm. Is the price the same?

A No, it'd be about ten percent higher for an equivalent craft due to the costs of importing and that sort of thing.

B I see. Seems doubtful in that case.

A Well, thank you very much.

1 No.   **2** Four to five thousand pounds.
3 So his children can get used to sailing when they're young.   **4** Twenty-five miles.   **5** No.

Focus on Language 2

1 as   **2** so that   **3** would mean   b due to

Listening for information 3

Mary Rogers	Hello.
Michelle Bernardon	Mary?
Mary Rogers	Hello, Michelle. How're things?
Michelle Bernardon	Not too good. You know this new category two model?
Mary Rogers	Oh, yes, *The Cutter*.
Michelle Bernardon	Well, one of of our main components manufacturers has got big problems.
Mary Rogers	Which manufacturer?
Michelle Bernardon	Well, you know we were sub-contracting the woodwork and fittings . . .
Mary Rogers	Yes.
Michelle Bernardon	. . . A small company, Peterson and Roberts. Highly specialised. Anyway, they won't be able to deliver on time for the London boat show. That means I must cancel our stand.
Mary Rogers	But can't you exhibit your present lines? I mean they've been . . .
Michelle Bernardon	No. You see, Mary, we planned to exhibit only sailing boats this year. Our category one prices are too high for the UK market. We only sold 42 last year.
Mary Rogers	But if you cancel your stand, you'll lose credibility and you know what that could lead to.
Michelle Bernardon	Yes, but look. In order to get *The Cutter* to the Boat Show we'd have to find another company and get them to do a rush job on the woodwork and fittings. That'd cost the earth.
Mary Rogers	Yes, but you know how much a lost deposit on a cancelled stand is – £1,000 and it's less than six weeks to go now.

Michelle Bernardon	Hmm . . . there is that.
Mary Rogers	Look, why don't you have a second try with both categories. Bring over a motor boat as well. At least it would mean that you wouldn't be forgotten on the UK market and then next year . . .
Michelle Bernardon	
Mary Rogers	

1 They won't be able to deliver for the Boat Show.
2 no   **3** no   **4** To get *The Cutter* to the Boat Show.
5 That'd cost the earth (That would . . .)
6 Why don't you have a second try with both categories (bring over a second boat as well)

Focus on Language 3

1 means   **2** could lead to   **3** In order to
4 it would mean that

PRACTICE 3

Model version

We're thinking of cancelling our stand at the Boat Show because of a delivery problem. As you know, we like to work with specialists and so we contract out quite a lot of work. But this means total dependence on them and unfortunately on this occasion Peterson and Roberts haven't been able to deliver on time. However, not exhibiting at the Boat Show could result in loss of credibility. Then again, we must bear in mind that our category one prices are too high for the UK market, which meant that we only sold 42 last year. Anyway, I don't think we should have a stand just to exhibit those boats alone.

On the other hand, I am aware that cancelling now will lead to the loss of our deposit which is a lot of money – £1,000.